# HOT RODS & CUSTOMS
## of the
## 1970s

Andy Southard Jr.

MBI Publishing Company

## Dedication

This book is dedicated to my son and daughter. They often reminisce about the wonderful times we had together enjoying rod runs and car club picnics. Sitting on their father's '32 Ford roadster running board are six-year-old Ericka (left) and two-year-old Aric (right). This picture was taken October 1, 1972, at Toro Park, in Salinas, California. We were the guests of Rod Powell, a well-known painter and customizer, who was having his annual picnic and get-together.

First published in 1998 by MBI Publishing Company, PO Box 1, 729 Prospect Avenue, Osceola, WI 54020-0001 USA

MBI Publishing Company books are also available at discounts in bulk quantity for industrial or sales-promotional use. For details write to Special Sales Manager at Motorbooks International Wholesalers & Distributors, 729 Prospect Avenue, PO Box 1, Osceola, WI 54020-0001 USA.

Library of Congress Cataloging-in-Publication Data
Southard, Andy.
    Hot rods & customs of the 1970s/Andy Southard, Jr.
        p. cm.
        Includes index.
        ISBN 0-7603-0536-6 (alk. paper)
    1. Hot rods—United States—History. 2. Automobiles—Customizing—United States—History. I. Title.
TL236.3.S674        1998
629.228'6'0973—dc2198-8467

**On the front cover:** When I took this picture of Gary and Marilyn Meadows' chop-top '32 Ford Tudor sedan in March 1977, they were members of the Danville Dukes Car Club. It was painted a beautiful yellow pearl by Gary Meadows and Lenny Mendes with black pinstriping by Tom's Signs as a finishing touch.

Under the hood is a 350-ci '67 Chevy, with a Holley carb on an Edelbrock manifold and a Mallory distributor. The transmission is a Chevy Powerglide, with 3.80 gears from a Ford rear end. Chrome wire wheels from a Buick Skylark add sparkle to the Pirelli tires. The front brakes are Pontiac and rear brakes are Ford.

Gary Meadows still has this yellow sedan, but it is nonfendered. Meadows is president of the Good Guys organization.

**On the frontispiece:** I began pinstriping in the 1950s, and still had a steady hand to carry on my decorative art into the 1990s. You can see my work on Rudy Heredia's '32 Ford roadster grille shell. Patterns of silver and emerald green complement the acrylic metallic green paint. Note my signature and the date on the shell, a standard practice of a pinstriper.

Heredia's roadster is pictured several times in this book. My previous books featured other fantastic cars that Heredia owned through the years.

**On the title page:** Customizer Gene Winfield of Modesto, California, created and built LeRoy Kemmerer's '56 Mercury in 1959. It was sectioned 4 inches, using '59 Chrysler rear quarter panels, matching wheel openings, and '57 Dodge front fender flares.

The car later was damaged in an accident, and afterward the top was replaced and body work was redone.

In this March 1979 picture, new owner Jerry Rehn of Salinas, California, has just completed the restoration, which included a re-creation of the Winfield candy-green paint job by Rod Powell of Salinas. With a tripod assist, I got into the picture with Jerry. I was very pleased to photograph the *Jade Idol* for *Hot Rod* magazine's *Rod & Custom 1979 Pictorial*.

**On the contents page:** In my previous book, *Hot Rods & Customs of the 1960s*, I had a picture of Neal East and myself trading ownership certificates for our roadsters.

Here is a picture of Neal's black '32 Ford roadster after it was torn down and rebuilt. A special bright red paint was selected, as were custom side panels, louvers, whitewall tires, 283-ci Chevy engine, automatic transmission, Ford station wagon rear end, and coil spring suspension.

I was a member of the Bay Area Roadster Club, and was lucky enough to drive Neal's car many pleasurable miles.

**On the back cover:** Ken Gwaltney of Culver City, California, owned this 3 1/2-inch chop-top '32 Ford coupe, photographed in the parking lot of the 11th Annual L.A. Roadsters Car Show and Swap Meet, June 15, 1975.

Providing the power was a 350-ci Chevy engine mated to a four-speed transmission, with a '57 Oldsmobile rear end. The front axle is dropped and chromed. The brakes are from a '40 Ford. Wishbones are chromed and split. Wheel Specialties manufactured the chrome wire wheels.

Jack Garrison of Kal Kustom Upholstery completed the fabric and black Naugahyde interior. The flames by Larry Wood and Leo Noviello were accomplished with acrylic paint.

It was rumored that the coupe was sold to Jeff Beck of Sussex, England, one of Europe's best rock 'n' roll guitarists.

**On the back cover, inset:** This shot of John D'Agostino's '51 Mercury was taken in the parking lot at Rod Powell's shop in August 1978. The Mercury was chopped 4 inches and had many body modifications, including slanted doorposts. Originally pearl-white, it was repainted a custom-mix purple to become a famous show car, the *Midnight Sensation*.

Edited by Dan Burger

Printed in Hong Kong through World Print, Ltd.

# Contents

Acknowledgments                                          6

Preface                                                  6

Chapter 1    *1970-1972*                                 9

Chapter 2    *1973-1974*                                47

Chapter 3    *1975-1976*                                69

Chapter 4    *1977-1979*                                97

             Index                                     128

# Acknowledgments

First off, I would like to thank MBI Publishing Company for the faith in me to do another book. It has been fun, nostalgic, and a pleasure to go through my archives and select color and black and white photos for this, my fourth book. Editor Keith Mathiowetz of MBI Publishing Company is exemplary in his support of my efforts. He also puts up with all my phone calls and inquiries, and my ramblings about the 1970s.

I also thank all of the people who have bought my other books, *Custom Cars of the 1950s, Hot Rods of the 1950s,* and *Hot Rods & Customs of the 1960s.* Your flattering letters are forever appreciated. Some of you have followed my writing and photography through magazines and books for the past 40-some years. It's always been a pleasure.

A very special thanks to my wife, Patty, who has had to live, eat, and breathe while constantly hearing about the 1970s. She's been through this before with other decades. She's a special gal, and I'm glad we can share the same interests together.

Again, I must acknowledge my long-time buddies. Through their association, I learned about cars and enjoyed them. They are Willie Wilde, Johnny Clegg, and Bill Acker of Florida, and Ken Fleischmann, Bernard "Izzy" Davidson, Chuck Thuren, and Bob Kraus of New York.

Much research has gone into this book—identifying cars and people. Assistance was given by Ed Lee, Jim Holland, Ralph Ferriera, Ralph "Rockin Ralph" Palmer, Red and Lee Ann Spence, Tom Cutino, Sherm Porter, Greg Sharp, Bill Moeller, Clyde Smith, Rod Powell, John D'Agostino, Mike Haas, Art Himsl, Joe Bailon, Don Tognotti, Rick Perry, Vince Burgos, Pat Ganahl, and Bob Schoonhoven—all Californians; Bob Kraus and Chuck Thuren of New York; Albert Drake and Paul Smith of Oregon; Darryl Starbird of Oklahoma; Bob Knowles of Arizona; Neal East of Colorado; and Norm Grabowski of Arkansas. And if I've forgotten anyone, you know who you are, and I thank you.

# Preface

Once again, MBI Publishing Company asked me to dig into my massive photo archives and put another book together. This time I decided to do the 1970s.

At first, the 1970s sounded like it was only yesterday. I thought maybe the subject matter is too new. But then I thought again. That decade began more than 25 years ago. When I took these pictures, many of the readers of this book weren't even born yet. They have never seen those times. And I also thought you older readers may enjoy having your memories jogged a little bit, too.

The hot rods and customs of the 1970s were not 1970-model cars. Most were 1950s and 1960s models styled in the 1970s fashion. Customizers were still lowering, molding, and chopping, as they had in the 1960s. The roadsters, coupes, and sedans were so radically altered and accessorized with 1970s-era components. Paint jobs were still lavish, and the favorites were the scallops, pearls, candies, and the ever-popular flame pattern.

Not all the cars in this book were built for individual owners. Some are "gimmick" cars—built for the car show circuits with outlandish styling meant to entice the younger generation. Among them are the specialty cars built for the television programs—the *Mork and Mindy* egg-shaped *Morque Machine,* designed by Larry Wood, and built by Rod Powell for Group Promotions, and Revelle's pink pearl *Charlie's Angels* Chevy van, another Rod Powell production.

You will also notice that the popularity of pickup trucks carried into the 1970s. Pickup clubs were organized with names such as the California Stepsides. Some of these pickups were only moderately customized, while others were chopped, lowered, and painted with incredible designs and colors. A few examples are shown in this book, treated as a form of custom cars.

All the photos in this book were taken during the 1970s. They were printed from my original black and white negatives and color slides. Most of them were 35 millimeter, but a few were photographed with a 2 1/4-inch format camera. I also shot some black and white photos and made those prints myself. I still use the same Hasselblad camera today.

When I began reviewing my color pictures for this book, I found 5,001 pictures, which I narrowed down to a more workable 460 photos. Then came the hard part—the frustrating task of choosing the 142 color pictures that are in this book.

The easy part was during the 1970s, when I was a member of the Bay Area Roadster Club. I traveled many miles participating in club functions and while at these events, I photographed many of the cars that are shown on the following pages.

I took pictures of these hot rods and customs for my enjoyment, not for any historical record. It turns out to be a personal photographic record of my times and what I loved to photograph. I hope you enjoy them and my personal experiences that serve as captions.

I must thank all of you who have written to me over the years. Some have even telephoned to tell me how much you have enjoyed my pictures and what I have photographed.

You will see, throughout this book, that most of the photography originated in events that were prevalent during the 1970s. A couple of my favorites were Andy Brizio's "Hot Rod" picnic get-togethers, the Los Angeles Roadster Club Father's Day car shows and swap meets of 1970 and 1975, the first Lodi "Mini-Nationals" of 1973, the L.A. Roadsters and the Bay Area Roadsters get-together in San Luis Obispo in 1974, and the Roadster Roundups. I have some coverage of shows at Oakland, San Mateo, San Jose, and the L.A. Winternationals.

Many of the customs and hot rods of the 1970s were built by guys who had been doing that work since the 1950s. Some who are still doing it today include Bill Cushenbery, George Barris, Bill Hines, Gene Winfield, Dean Jeffries, Larry Watson, and Darryl Starbird.

Among the many cars that I photographed, a few of my favorites were designed by extremely talented enthusiasts. Among these I would include Tom Prufer's '29 Ford roadster and his outstanding Ford T track-style flamed roadster; Don Varner's '29 Ford roadster pickup; and his '23 Ford T track-style roadster. Varner would later win the "America's Most Beautiful Roadster" award (Oakland Roadster Show) in 1984 for his *California Star* aluminum-bodied roadster, a car well ahead of its time.

Other favorites include a couple by "The Rodfather," Andy Brizio. His '23 Ford *Instant T* roadster won the "America's Most Beautiful Roadster" award in 1970. Years later he came up with another T style, the C-cab. These rods were fantastic.

Another two-time award winner was John Corno of Portland, Oregon. I have photos of his first winner, a fantastic '28 Ford highboy roadster, and his second winner as well, a rear-engined '30 Model A Ford roadster.

In case you think that photographing cars is all hard work, please note that many times there were models posing with the cars that I photographed. These wholesome-looking girls often wore titles such as Miss San Bruno or Miss Brisbane. Through the courtesy of nightclub owner Voss Boreta, I had the pleasure of photographing Carol Doda, the acclaimed San Francisco nightclub entertainer. This line of work sometimes has its uniquely interesting moments.

I'm proudest of the photo with Bob Hirohata and his legendary one-of-a-kind customized '51 Mercury coupe crafted by Barris Kustoms. I first met Hirohata in Barris' shop in 1958, when Barris was installing Appleton spotlights on my '58 Chevy. This photo was taken in the mid-1970s and was later autographed in 1978. It is one of my prized possessions.

I retired in April 1998, after working for 36 years with the Monterey County Public Works Department. I plan to take a short vacation, and hopefully continue to do more books for Motorbooks International.

I hope you will enjoy *Hot Rods & Customs of the 1970s*, with my pictures and captions, along with historical trivia and recollections of my experiences. Your thoughts and comments, as always, will be welcome.

*Andy Southard Jr.*
*5 San Juan Drive*
*Salinas, California 93901-3012*

# Chapter

# 1 1970-1972

As the 1960s spilled into the 1970s, the war in Vietnam had become the longest armed conflict in U.S. history. The battles in Southeast Asia had cost more than 30,000 lives, and the protests here were causing great strife within the country. In January 1970, Lt. Everett Alvarez set an American record for the longest time spent as a prisoner of war—2,000 days.

Richard Nixon was president, but not for long. The Beatles were still making the most popular music, yet they would break up quicker than the Nixon administration. The biggest movie event of 1970 starred bulldog-tough George C. Scott in his unforgettable role as World War II hero General Patton.

The Super Bowl was still an infant. The 1970 clash between Kansas City and Minnesota was the last one played between the rival leagues before the merger. The KC victory is remembered less than the Vikings' defeat—the first of four upset losses that would haunt the franchise to this day.

Al Unser, driving the *Johnny Lightning 500 Special*, won the 1970 Indy 500. It was the first of two consecutive wins at the Brickyard for Unser and the first of his four checkered flags there.

In the evolution of the all-American hot rod, something entirely un-American was going on. Rear end components from an expensive British car, the

Oakland Roadster Show's "America's Most Beautiful Roadster" of 1970 belonged to South San Fransciscan Andy Brizio.

His creation was powered by a 301-ci '57 Chevy with an Iskenderian 440 cam and a 4.71 GMC supercharger linked to an Edelbrock manifold and Carter AFB four-barrel carb. Custom headers were made by Sanderson. Horsepower was reported to be 450. The transmission is a B & M Automotive Street & Drag with a 3.70 rear end ratio.

Upholstery is brown leather with nylon carpets by O. C. Mack of Sacramento. Steve Archer made the replica '23 Ford body from fiberglass, and Art Himsl of Concord, California, painted the psychedelic-looking lacquer, using separate hues of pastels over pearl.

Suspension is by leaf springs in the front and coil springs in the rear, with Monroe tube shocks all around. The extensive chrome-plating was done by C & M Plating. Modeling next to Oakland's 9-foot trophy is Debbrah Henley, Miss San Bruno.

Bay Area Roadster Club member Rudy Heredia of Gilroy, California, owned this '32 Ford roadster. The metallic green acrylic paint job was by Rudy and Larry's Body Shop of Gilroy, and the black Naugahyde upholstery is credited to Banning, also of Gilroy. Heredia made the custom dash with Stewart Warner gauges.

Most of the car's undercarriage is chromed, with dropped front axle, '40 Ford spindles and brakes, and chromed Delco tube shocks. Goodyear tires are mounted on Ansen Sprint wheels.

The engine is a 283-ci '67 Chevy, sporting Hedman headers, Edelbrock intake manifold, and Rochester carbs. The transmission is a '64 Chevy four-speed hooked up to a '56 Pontiac rear end, narrowed 6 1/2 inches.

The firewall holds dual master cylinders that operate both clutch and brakes. Air filters are polished aluminum boat flame arrestors, which were popular at that time.

Jaguar XKE, were becoming common. Their coil-over-shocks suspension and disc brakes formed a compact unit and became a "trick" application used by many top rod-builders. Another trend that would take off in the 1970s was the profusion of chrome-plated engine and suspension parts. It seemed that all that glitters must be chrome.

The High Performance and Custom Trade Show in Anaheim, California, in only its fourth year of existence in 1970, was on its way to becoming one of the biggest annual events on the hot rod and custom calendar. This event—now held in Las Vegas, Nevada, and known as the SEMA/AI Show—has become the "must-see" exhibition of companies that provide automotive aftermarket accessories.

Another milestone in 1970 was the inaugural event known as the Rod & Custom Street Rod Nationals. This annual hobby happening took place in August in Peoria, Illinois.

Individual highlights from this era of hot rodding include Vic Hawkins picking up the "Sam Barris" award, for the best body and paint work on a metal body, at the 1971 Sacramento Autorama with his excellent '37 Ford pickup truck. Winners at the prestigious Oakland Roadster show were Andy Brizio with his *Instant T*, '23 Ford roadster in 1970; Lonnie Gilbertson with a '23 Ford T roadster in 1971; and John Corno with a '30 Ford rear-engined roadster in 1972.

The car show season usually opened with the San Mateo Autorama, produced by Harry Costa.

On January 10, 1970, Rich Salice's '29 Ford roadster pickup made an appearance representing the Bay Area Roadster Club.

Salice's engine is a 354-ci '55 Chrysler featuring Jahns pistons, Delong camshaft, ported and polished heads, and Weiand intake manifold with dual AFB carbs. The transmission is a Chevy four-speed with Hurst linkage; the rear end is from a '49 Oldsmobile.

In front is a dropped axle with stock leaf springs, '48 Ford spindles, and Hurst Airheart disc brakes. Goodyear tires are on Ansen wheels.

Stock seating is retained even though the body is channeled 3 inches over the frame. The black Naugahyde upholstery is by Banning of Gilroy, and the Titian red paint is by Flyers Body Shop of San Jose.

Master craftsman Steve Archer built this '23 T touring car for his bikini-clad wife, Arlene. In this April 1970 photo, Arlene is modeling and Steve is giving his seal of approval. (Check out that smile!) The Archers lived in San Bruno, California, where Steve was in the business of building fiberglass roadster and touring bodies.

Archer custom-built the headers to fit the 1968 Ford 289 engine, gave the T body its starburst blue paint, and built the teakwood running boards. Bob Epperson of San Bruno did the upholstery in Natural brown DuPont Koraseal.

The '23 touring weighed 1,870 pounds and went through the quarter mile in 13.2 seconds at 97 miles per hour. Steve passed away in November 1997.

Joe Palmer, a member of the San Jose Roadster Club, owned this beautiful '32 Ford roadster. The Tahitian red lacquer was applied by Mel Fisher of Palo Alto, with white pinstriping by Neil Averill.

Under the hood is a 327-ci '65 Chevy, with an automatic transmission behind it. The rear end and suspension was XKE Jaguar, a popular item on rods of this vintage. Les Erben machined the hubs to accept Buick Skylark wire wheels, on which are mounted narrow Firestone DeLuxe Champion tires.

The dashboard was original, but extra gauges and switches were mounted to a panel on the floor. Black Naugahyde upholstery was by Burke's Auto Upholstery of Redwood City.

This replica 1917 Model T was made into a 96-inch wheelbase roadster pickup by Wilson Farrell of the Townsmen Car Club of Sacramento, California.

The T is built on a 2x3-inch Z-tube frame, with the body channeled 3 inches over the frame. Pearl-yellow paint combines nicely with the black 1970s cob webbing and pinstriping by Ivan Page. Vern Hunter did the diamond-tufted black Naugahyde and nylon rugs. The pickup bed houses an eight-gallon gas tank.

The engine is a 301-ci '59 Chevy, with Duntov 30-30 cam, fuel-injection pistons, and 600-series Holleys on top of a Edelbrock high-riser manifold. It makes use of a three-speed transmission, and a chromed '57 Chevy rear end.

The Roadsters of L.A. and *Rod & Custom* magazine presented the Sixth Annual Roadster Exhibition and Swap Meet, June 21, 1970, at the Great Western Exhibit Center.

L.A. Club member Lanny Boeltl of Whittier, California, owned this '31 Ford roadster pickup, built with '32 Ford frame, fenders and bumpers, and a '29 Ford pickup bed. Boeltl chopped the windshield 2 inches and did his own black crushed-grain Naugahyde upholstery.

The front end has a dropped axle, and '40 Ford brakes are fitted all around. Power comes from a '48 Mercury flathead with a 1/4-inch-stroke crankshaft. Other goodies include a Weber cam, Jahns pistons, Offenhauser heads, and Evans intake manifold with three Stromberg carbs. The transmission is a '39 Ford with Lincoln Zephyr gears and a Schiefer clutch. The instrumentation features Stewart Warner gauges.

Wanna buy a '27 Ford Tudor sedan? Under the multilouvered hood was a 153-ci engine from a '62 Chevy II, backed up with a Powerglide transmission.

It is set up with Kinmont disc brakes, Red Kelsey-Hayes wire wheels, a dropped axle, and 5.00x16 Goodyear tires up front with 7.50x16 in the rear, which gives the car its smart rake. Check out the vintage T steering wheel.

Owner Bo Jones of Van Nuys, California, was showing his classy Tangerine '27 in the parking lot of the Roadster Exhibition and Swap Meet at the Great Western Exhibit Center.

Andy Brizio, one of the great builders of this era, is also remembered for hosting some memorable parties. This shot was taken at his fourth annual picnic, held at Crow Canyon Park, Castro Valley, California, on August 2, 1970. Andy's picnic, equivalent to the Roadster Roundup or the L.A. Roadster Exhibition, was an outstanding array of coupes, sedans, roadsters, and customs.

This '39 Chevy two-door sedan belonging to well-known painter and customizer Rod Powell, was painted pearl-yellow with candy-green flames and orange pinstriped edges.

Rod's Chevy was sectioned and channeled 4 inches over the frame, with a flair added to the rear fender wells. He kept the original taillights, but the bumpers were removed and the headlights were molded to the fenders. Goodyear tires are mounted on '53 Buick wire wheels.

Under the hood is a '57 Chevy engine, backed by a three-speed transmission and '57 Chevy rear end.

Also from the Brizio picnic is this '41 Chevy custom coupe, a Gold Medal winner at the '72 Oakland Show. It is owned by Paul McElley and was modeled after a similar custom owned by Joe Bailon, another picnic regular.

McElley's car was stripped of chrome, had molded quarter windows, and the hood was nosed. The grille is from a Buick, and the frenched headlights are from a Studebaker. Note how the trunk opening was molded along with the rear splash panel. The bumper was flipped upside down. The tunneled and frenched '59 Cadillac taillight lenses were another nice touch, as was the blue crushed-velvet interior fabric.

14

**R**alph Ferreira, a hot rodder from Salinas, California, did all his own work on this '23 T fiberglass Ford roadster pickup, installing a 327-ci Chevy engine with a high-rise Weiand manifold and Holley 750 carb. Outside-type headers were created by Sanderson of San Francisco.

The transmission is a Chevy Powerglide, hooked up to a '56 Oldsmobile rear end on a frame made of 2x3-inch steel tubing, using a '32 Ford front end with a chromed dropped axle. All four brakes were from a '40 Ford. The top-mounted coil springs, front tube-shocks, and front axle were plated by Joe the Chromer of Salinas.

Ferreira laid on the pearl-green paint job himself, and Manger of Castroville did the black Naugahyde interior and top.

**G**eorge Solimine of South San Francisco, California, owned this cherry '32 Ford three-window coupe. It was painted acrylic Rio red, with "Tommy the Greek" black-and-white pinstriping. Body alterations include 34 louvers in the hood and a filled grille shell.

Under the hood is a 283-ci '58 Chevy, sporting Hedman exhaust headers and an Edelbrock manifold with six Stromberg 97 carburetors. A '39 Ford transmission runs Lincoln Zephyr gears, with a closed driveshaft to a '41 Ford rear end.

Up front is a '32 Ford axle that is dropped 3 inches, and Columbus tube shocks. Brakes, all around, are from a '48 Ford. The rolling stock is made up of popular American mag wheels—7-inch in front, 8 1/2-inch in the rear—with Goodyear tires. Mack of Sacramento did the black Naugahyde upholstery.

Ralph Ferreira shows his strength by lifting his brother's '23 Ford T Volks-rod.

Gilbert Ferreira powered his rod with a 1,600-cc Volkswagen engine stationed in the pickup bed, creating a fairly light front end. The suspension setup features torsion bars and friction shocks on a 4130 chrome-moly tube chassis. The axle is a dropped tube. It runs on spoked American mag wheels with Pirelli tires. Firemist cinnamon lacquer paint and brown Naugahyde upholstery complete the picture.

In the background, to the left, are Gilbert Ferreira, Lorraine Ferreira, and Carl Johnson. Ralph Ferreira's '23 Ford roadster is to the right, and to the left is Carl Johnson's "Buick" roadster.

One outstanding touring car at the Fifth Annual Roadster Roundup, September 1970, in Visalia, California, was Rich and Dana Thompson's '24 Ford, with Fiber-Motive stretched fiberglass body. Lou Hislop of Santa Ana painted the car in jet-black lacquer with gold pinstriping. Stewart Warner gauges grace the custom dashboard.

The tall windshield was a product of Antique Auto Parts, the same company that supplied the 10-inch steering wheel. Upholstery is black button-tufted Naugahyde. This Ford is powered by a 215-ci Buick engine with Weber carburetion. The brakes are Hurst/Airheart discs, and the front axle has a full 4-inch drop executed by MAS Racing Products. Rich is a member of the L.A. Roadsters.

Proportions might look exaggerated on Milo Broz's sectioned coupe, but the trunk area is actually as thin as it looks. The trunk, which accommodates a spare tire and a minimum amount of luggage, is upholstered with black nylon carpet.

Taillights are stock '50 Ford. Rear fender wells were radiused high into the quarter panels to clear the G70x15 Firestone tires, mounted on chromed Buick wire wheels. Milo altered the '56 Buick bumpers himself and designed the '58 Ford Thunderbird bucket seats, covered in black Naugahyde and fabric by Jack's Auto Top of San Mateo.

A Naugahyde-covered console houses an air vent, heater, and switches. Pretty 19-year-old Debbie Wright, Miss Millbrae, graciously modeled for us.

As a teenager, Milo Broz of Burlingame, California, spent three years and $4,000 building this sectioned '50 Ford coupe, doing most of the work himself.

Milo took a 5 1/2-inch section from the middle of the coupe and made the black painted expanded metal grille by contouring a 1/2-inch plate to fit the frenched opening. Side trim is from a '55 Ford Fairlane. Jacopi's of Burlingame painted the Florentine Gold acrylic.

Under the hood is a 430-ci '58 Mercury with Crane cam and lifters and three Holley two-throat carburetors priming the pump. Milo made his own custom headers, and the '53 Hydra-matic transmission was built by B & M.

I first met Dennis Varni in February 1964, when he came to my house to get his orange '31 Ford roadster pinstriped in black. After the striping job, I took pictures for a feature in the August 1964 issue of *Rod & Custom* magazine.

His '29 Ford roadster, newly completed in September 1970, was built on a '32 Ford frame with a '29 roadster body, finished in American La France red paint with Tommy the Greek black-and-white pinstriping. Mechanics include a 327-ci Chevy with a Borg Warner T-10 transmission, '57 Olds rear end, and '56 Ford pickup truck steering.

A Action Auto in Sacramento did the buckskin Naugahyde and tan nylon interior. Dennis is a long-time member of the B.A.R. club.

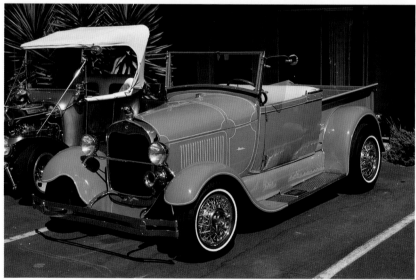

The Fifth Roadster Roundup in Visalia was in full swing on Saturday, September 12, 1970. One of the beauties on display was this '29 Ford roadster pickup, owned by L.A. Roadster member Carl Riggen of Los Angeles, and rebuilt by his brother-in-law, the famous Dick "Magoo" Megugorac. The engine is a 327-ci Chevy, with a Powerglide transmission mated to a Jaguar rear end and suspension. The front axle is a dropped Bell-style, and front brakes are Airheart discs on special caliper mounting plates.

The paint is '56 Thunderbird peacock blue, with white pinstriping. Arco Upholstery of Woodland Hills completed the Naugahyde and woven cloth interior. The chromed wire wheels are from an early Thunderbird. An extra-large gas tank is fitted under the pickup bed.

I took this picture of Dick Scritchfield on October 3, 1970, during the Los Angeles/Bay Area Roadster get-together at Moro Bay. The photo he is holding shows his "highboy" '32 Ford at the 22nd Annual Bonneville National Speed Trials. The roadster ran 159.485 miles per hour in a newly created, complete street roadster class—a record he later broke with a 165.327-mile per hour run in the new C/STR street roadster class. Dick's highboy was powered by a 350-ci Chevy.

Sam Conrad's cool-looking, non-fendered '29 Ford roadster, photographed at the Visalia Roadster Roundup in 1970, was painted a dark-blue acrylic lacquer. The interior, by Eddie Martinez, was nicely done with small pleats in pearl-white Naugahyde. The custom dash included six Stewart Warner gauges, and the firewall was covered with mahogany.

A 2 1/2-inch chromed dropped axle with '48 Ford spindles and '40 Ford brakes figured into the front end setup, along with big and little tires, Halibrand wheels, and custom hairpin split wishbones.

An awesome 483-ci Oldsmobile with six Stromberg carbs and chromed custom outside-type headers gave this rod a real presence. They sounded great when un-plugged!

The roadster is still around, belonging to Bob Gorby of Indiana, but now it's Chevy powered.

Jeff and Judy Wussow's '23 T touring won "Best Appearing Car" at the Visalia Roadster Roundup. It wears Roman red lacquer and is pin-striped in white by the famous "Von Dutch." The black Naugahyde interior and top were the work of Bob Lindebaum.

Crammed under the hood is a 289-ci Ford with all the accessories: Flex-A-Lite fan, alternator, and a radiator that uses upper and lower tanks with a late-model core. Up front are a chromed PSI axle with the steering arm, radius rods and spindles from a '48 Ford, and Hurst/Airheart disc brakes. A Jaguar provided the rear end and Chrysler the wire wheels, wearing Michelin radials.

This photo was taken at the 1970 Los Angeles/Bay Area Roadster Meet at Moro Bay.

One of the semicustoms at the 1971 San Mateo Autorama was John D'Agostino's 1970 Pontiac Grand Prix, awarded "Class Champion" honors throughout the 1970-1971 International Show Car Association (ISCA) season. The 19-year-old from Pittsburg, California, bought the car new. Ed Fry of Mr. Ed's Body Shop in Concord did the front and rear lowering and the body work. The narrow double-whitewall tires on chromed wire wheels and the white angel hair surrounding the display made a real styling statement.

John had the Art Himsl/Mike Haas Custom Paint Studio of Concord paint the candy gold with tangerine blends. Ken Foster of Sacramento did the black Naugahyde interior, with Parfait Butterscotch carpets.

Lonnie Gilbertson, a machinist from Portland, Oregon, literally hand-built this '23 T fiberglass roadster pickup, using a handmade rectangular tube frame with PSI dropped tube front axle on transverse leaf springs, homemade hubs, and disc brakes by H & H Calipers.

A 327-ci '68 Chevy is topped with a Moon intake manifold holding four Weber 48 IDA carbs. Gilbertson fabricated a set of headers that exit just in front of the rear wheels. The automatic transmission is backed up with a '66 Jaguar XKE rear end. Phil Clark made the aluminum hood. Lonnie and brother Gary prepared the body, then had pearl-red lacquer applied by Frank & Dave's Auto Paint.

It was awarded "America's Most Beautiful Roadster" at the 23rd Annual Oakland Roadster Show in February 1971.

Another winner at the Oakland Roadster Show of 1971 was Spud DeCruz of Hayward, California, whose '51 Mercury coupe won first in his class.

Lowering the Merc 3 1/2 inches in rear and 4 inches up front was a nice move.

The Goodyears up front were 4.50x15, while 10.50x15s were worn on the rear. The rubber was mounted on silver-painted wheels with chrome beauty rings. Rear fender wells were radiused 4 inches for more clearance. Ron Laconi straightened the body and partially de-chromed the nose of the hood. This paint is metallic plum acrylic lacquer.

Continental Plating of Oakland rechromed the grille, bumpers, and emblems. Cardero Brothers in Mexico did the black Naugahyde upholstery, which features 2-inch pleats on seats and side panels. The window reveals and dashboard were sprayed with black lacquer. The engine, transmission, and rear end are stock.

I had so much fun photographing this outstanding '29 Ford roadster, owned by San Francisco's "Off Broadway" night club owner and entrepreneur, Voss Boreta, that within a couple of hours I took more than 125 pictures in black and white and color.

This Malayan red, hand-rubbed lacquered roadster body sits on a black-painted '32 Ford chassis. Airheart disc brakes are fitted to a chromed '34 Ford axle that is dropped 4 inches. Hairpin wishbones are split and chromed. The '34 Ford steering gear is a modified pitman arm design. Goodyear tires sit on Cragar wheels.

A & A Top & Trim of San Francisco fitted the black Naugahyde pleated upholstery. Eight Stewart Warner gauges fill the dash. Sitting behind the wheel is Voss Boreta, accompanied by model Carol Doda.

Voss Boreta's roadster is powered by a 454-ci Chrysler engine, which is force-fed by a 671 GMC blower with dual carbs, driven to a 1-to-1 ratio. The engine is coupled to a B & M TorqueFlite transmission, which leads to a chromed '60 Mercury rear end with 4.30 gears. A closer look shows chrome tube shocks, Dietz 820 headlights, and close-fitting cycle fenders.

Voss brought Carol Doda, a famous night club entertainer, to pose with his roadster. Carol, in her '70s-style white bikini and tall white boots, was very popular.

As you can see, the front end of Tom Prufer's tangerine pearl '29 Ford roadster is all chromed, including the Deitz 820 lights and custom brackets. Pete Ogden made the aluminum hood and side panels, which include 98 louvers. The windshield and posts were chopped 3 inches.

Ken Foster of Sacramento is responsible for the tan pleated interior. 1967 Pontiac slit taillights are on the rear lower panel.

That's Tom in the driveway, checking out his Jaguar disc brakes. The XKE rear end setup was done by Joe "XKE" Cardoza.

Tom Prufer's '29 Ford roadster, minus the hood and side panels, shows off the 289-ci Ford that sits in its '32 Ford frame. Prominent is a big four-barrel carb and a Joe Hunt Magneto. The transmission is a C-4.

Edelbrock aluminum finned valve covers enhance the engine compartment. Pete Ogden made the chromed headers, as well as the fan and pulleys. Notice indications of small ghost flames on the top and side of the cowling.

Split wishbones are nicely made and chromed. Polished Ansen wheels are fitted with Goodyear tires. Polished stainless steel soft drink canisters in the trunk serve as a gas tank. Stainless steel floor pan is also polished.

At the 1971 Oakland Roadster Show, this roadster was a Silver Medal winner.

This 1937 Ford pickup, owned by Vic Hawkins, was the best of show at the Sacramento Autorama in 1971. Hawkins rebuilt the truck himself in the course of three years.

In the process, he replaced the stock engine with a '40 Ford V-8, installed a column-shift transmission, and a Ford rear end. The engine received Weiand high-compression heads, an Edelbrock manifold with three chromed 97 carburetors, porcelain exhaust headers, a chromed fan, and a dual clutch/brake master cylinder on the firewall.

The interior features dark-brown Naugahyde upholstery in a hexagonal pattern and dark-brown rugs. Toggle switches on the dash operate lights and electric windows. The flooring in the bed of the truck is walnut, as is the outer face of the tailgate. The luscious paint is pearl yellow with gold-brown highlights. I like those Firestone Wide Oval tires mounted on Cadillac wire wheels.

At the 21st Sacramento Autorama, Vic won the coveted "Sam Barris" award, and overall sweepstakes for the best car of show. After all these years, Vic still has his pickup. The picture is dated April 3, 1971.

The *Playbunny Coach*, photographed here in 1971, was created from a '55 Chevy Nomad show car that I photographed at the San Mateo Autorama in 1968.

Mike and Eric Erickson sectioned the Nomad body 8 inches, chopped the top 4 inches, and installed an Olds Vista Cruiser upper roof. A roof-mounted air foil provides a special effect. The *Playbunny Coach* also has a tilt front end that hinges from the firewall forward. Highlighting the custom handiwork was a grille formed from sheet metal and chromed, hand-built headlight buckets, and notched fenders that opened to the side to route the exhaust headers and side pipes.

The power source is a 409 Chevy, with GMC blower, custom outside exhausts, and a B & M Hydra-matic.

Mike Haas painted the *Playbunny Coach* a candy red, with honey gold and darker gold highlights.

Ken Foster of A Action Interiors of Sacramento fashioned the upholstery in red velvet. The custom dash contained a built-in radio and TV where the glove box would have been and a front console housed a phone. The shortened rear deck lid and window open in the normal fashion. The rear portion of the interior had no seat, but the flat area was padded and upholstered.

Taillight housings are from a '55 Chevy, with a custom one-piece plastic lens. The chromed wheels, with knock-off hubs, are from a '66 Buick Riviera. On the rear the rims are 18 inches deep, with Dunlop Racing tires.

A rear grille opening was frenched, and expanded metal was used in the background.

**A**t the 1971 Rod & Custom Street Rod Nationals in Memphis, Tennessee, Andy Brizio's *Instant T* C-cab won the "Best Appearing Car" trophy, an award determined by car-owner voting.

I took these pictures six days before the car left for Memphis.

Jerry Stich and Ray Callejo fabricated the 112-inch wheelbase chassis in Andy's shop. For power, Andy used a 350-ci '71 Chevy engine with a 471 GMC blower, Fred Sanderson headers, and Joe Hunt magneto. The front end was chromed and a dropped tube axle was used. Jim Babb built the heavy-duty brass radiator. American mag wheels were fitted with Goodyear 7x15s on the front and 8 1/2x15s on the rear. The fiberglass body and hardwood bracing was the work of Steve Archer.

**B**rizio's T used a B & M Turbo-Hydramatic transmission, and the rear end is the popular XKE Jaguar type. Disc brakes were fitted all around.

T Hood Works of Moro Bay made the 1915 steel front fenders, but the rear fenders are 1916 vintage. Ken Foster of Sacramento did the brown wide-pleated Naugahyde upholstery. The walnut dash with Stewart Warner gauges was the work of Bob Burton. The gear selector, light switch, and a stereo are located in a seat riser under the driver.

Art Himsl painted the pearl white and multicolored hues, and his wife, Ellen, painted the characterizations of the people who helped Andy with his C-cab. The illustrated scroll depicts, in gold leaf, Route 66 from Los Angeles to Chicago. Art's portrait is on the rear door. Later, I was honored when a characterization of me in my roadster was painted on the driver-side panel.

This '61 Corvette, owned by Ted Mitchell of Salinas, California, was painted acrylic candy-wild cherry with pearl-white flames and striping. The talented Rod Powell did the painting, and Mitchell did the custom touches—removing the front emblem, blacking out the grille cavity, and installing GTO parking lights under the bumpers. He fashioned a small rear-deck-lid spoiler and used GTO taillight units; fender wells were flared and radiused. Goodyear tires were mounted on Ansen Sprints—10-inch rims on the rear, 8 1/2-inch on the front.

Howard's of Salinas completed the black Naugahyde upholstery in a square diamond-tufted pattern. Under the hood is a 283-ci '61 Chevy with factory dual-quad carburetion. This shot was taken at Rod Powell's 1971 "get-together" picnic at Toro Regional Park in Salinas.

Customizer Joe Bailon started this project with just two frame rails and some sketches made by designers Ed Newton and Bob Reisner. Six months later, he had the 28 1/2-foot long Pink Panther promotional car.

Bailon built a conduit framework, devised a steering system of individual screw jacks, and dropped in a '70 Olds Toronado engine and front-drive suspension. He shot the pink pearl paint himself. The upholstery was completed by Joe Perez, in the city of Commerce.

One of the participants in the 1971 Los Angeles Winternationals Car Show was Norm Grabowski of Sunland, California, with his jet-black '54 Ford F-100 pickup. Grabowski was a member of the Pick-Ups Limited of Southern California.

The F-100 was powered by a 283-ci Chevy, with a Turbo-Hydra-matic transmission connected to a Jaguar rear end. Front suspension was a '66 Dodge torsion-bar unit.

The top was chopped 3 inches, and the vent windows in the doors were eliminated. Brushed aluminum outlined the Von Dutch-built, aluminum egg-crate grille. The factory-style hood peak was hammered out smooth, and the headlight panels were custom made from sheet steel.

The insert picture caught Norm leaving the Los Angeles Convention and Exhibition Center after the show.

John Corno of Portland, Oregon, called his car The Roadster. I photographed it at the 1972 Oakland Roadster Show.

To begin this project, Corno had a '30 Ford roadster body shipped from Hawaii to custom builder Russ Meeks. The collaboration between those two resulted in this far-out rear-engined roadster. It could, by the way, be driven.

Meeks made the chassis from 2-inch chrome moly tubing. The water lines, brake lines, wiring, and fuel lines run through the chassis. To accommodate the rear-mounted 425-ci '68 Toronado engine, the body was lengthened 3 inches. Four Weber 48-millimeter carbs and a Crower hydraulic cam add muscle to the Olds mill.

Brass-plated Buick wire wheels and brown Mohair upholstery complement the metallic brown paint. The Roadster won the AMBR title in 1972. After it was shown at several shows, Russ bought the car from John.

I was with the Bay Area Roadsters at a roadster roundup in Visalia, California, in September 1969, when I met Greg Sharp, who was interested in finding a '29 Ford roadster pickup for sale.

I knew of one, told him all the details, and within a few weeks he bought it, and he still owns it today. We've been close friends ever since.

In this picture from 1972, Greg (left) and I are in my garage, when he was interviewing me for an article in Street Rod magazine. The object of our discussion, my Chevy-powered roadster, was a terrific driver, with an automatic transmission, late-model rear end, and disc brakes. The color was Naples orange, and the upholstery was black Naugahyde.

▲ 327-ci '62 Chevy with a Carter Thermoquad carb and Hedman headers lurks under the hood of this '33 Ford coupe, with a Muncie four-speed with a Hurst shifter control and a '56 Corvette 3.36 Posi-Traction rear end to get the rubber rolling.

Owner Tom Stryker of San Jose, California, did all his own body work. After he took the ripples and dents out, he had Anderson-Botel Cooperative Body Shop paint the black fenders and Cadillac Firefrost-green body. ABC Upholstery tailored his wide-pleated black Naugahyde interior.

The front end has stock springs and axle, but the brakes are '41 Ford. Stewart Warner gauges were substituted for the stock, and the glove box was reworked to fit a radio. Goodyear tires are wrapped around American mag wheels.

Also shown at the 1972 Oakland Roadster Show, in the full custom hardtop class, was Dave Miglietto's 1967 Ford Thunderbird, *Aladdin's Dream.*

Miglietto, who did a nice job with his body and paint work, chopped 7 1/2 inches from the top and redesigned it by eliminating the side quarter windows. The rear fenders were extended 8 inches, front and rear fender wells were flared, and custom taillights were added. The front end was narrowed 4 inches, and a recontoured, extended nose received a set-back mesh grille.

Miglietto painted the car white Murano pearl with black pinstriping, and Ken Foster and Jan Hunter of A Action Auto Interiors created the pearl red-and-white Naugahyde upholstery. Firestone tires and wheels came from Tognotti's Speed Shop in Sacramento.

Andy Brizio's "Home of the Instant T," on Old Mission Road in South San Francisco, is where most of Jerry Stich's 1915 Model T C-cab tow truck started.

This 1972 photograph shows Andy and unidentified others feverishly working on the truck to get it finished for the Street Rod Nationals, held that year in Detroit. There were 1,575 cars registered at the nationals and Stich's truck won "Best Appearing" and the "People's Choice" awards.

Andy Brizio is sitting in the cab, installing a windshield wiper motor.

The fabulous painting was done by Art Himsl of Concord, California. It is definitely a one-of-a-kind job, with pearl yellow-blue-white paint, and multicolored ribbons and murals.

The brown Naugahyde upholstery was done with wide pleats and buttons by Ken Foster of A Action Auto Interiors of Sacramento. Jerry crafted the bed and hoist system, with an electric super winch powering the chrome-plated towing mechanism and hoist.

The chromed rear end is from a Jaguar sedan, and the steering unit came from a VW bus. Frame construction is made up of 2x4-inch tubing. The front fenders are straight-type 1915 units from Howard Caccia of T Hood Works. Goodyear tires are mounted on American mags.

Jerry and his C-cab are joined by Miss Brisbane, 18-year-old Alice Gardner of Brisbane, California. Jerry's the one leaning over the engine compartment, in case you didn't already know that.

That's a 327-ci Chevy in the T. It has TRW rings, a Central Grinding cam, special heads by Ron, DC headers, and a 12-quart oil pan. Spark is by Accel Supercoil. An Andy's manifold mounts a 471 GMC blower with a Holley carburetor. Transmission is a Turbo-Hydra-matic, controlled by a B & M Hydra shifter. The engine was built by Cub Barnett.

The front end has a chromed 4-inch dropped axle and PSI hubs with disc brakes. The sealed-beam headlights are in the stock T housings. San Francisco's C & M Plating did all the chrome.

Looks like a stocker, doesn't it? Well, as we all know, looks can be deceiving. Tom Mierkey of Richmond, California, owned this '32 Ford three-window coupe, but his deuce only looks stock from the outside.

This car is gorgeous in every aspect, with a dropped-and-filled front axle, and a four-barrel 327-ci Corvette engine coupled to a Powerglide transmission. The rear end, including brakes, is from a '66 Corvette. Up front, the brakes are Ford hydraulics. Wide whitewall Firestone tires are mounted on chromed '56 Plymouth wire wheels.

The interior is upholstered in Mohair, while the rumble seat is done in tan Naugahyde. The dash contains instruments from a '33 Plymouth. Vans Auto Body of Berkeley painted the Chantilly poly maroon body and black fenders.

"Best Closed Car" at the Mid-State Rod Run in 1972 was Dan Eichstedt's Chevy-powered '34 Ford Tudor sedan. This black beauty stands only 50 inches high, requiring the seats to be channeled 2 inches into the floor pan.

The top has been chopped 3 1/2 inches, and the body has been sectioned 5 inches. Jim Jacobs and Pete Chapouris built the custom chassis that allowed such a low sedan. The fenders, grille, and hood needed extensive reworking to give the proper proportions and look.

A classic flame paint job was applied to the exterior, and velvet inserts are used with the black Naugahyde interior.

A total of 170 cars assembled for the Santa Barbara Rod Run, hosted by the Oldies-With-Goodies car club.

This channeled '32 Ford roadster is another 1950s-era custom brought back to life in the 1970s. It was originally built by Jerry Vrionis and, after being stored for more than 10 years, it was purchased by Dario Bucchianeri, a long-time friend.

Under the hood is a '57 Cadillac engine with dual 4-barrel carbs. Purposeful outside headers were made by Jerry and Charlie Tabucci, using mufflers from a Chrysler Imperial. A '48 Mercury donated the column, transmission, and rear end, as well as all the brakes. The front and rear tube shocks are from a '49 Plymouth.

Mercury wheels are a combination of chromed and painted black, with Goodyear tires. The dropped axle up front was chromed, and the headlights are Arrow sealed beams. Bright red Ford paint complements the black leather seats. There are 198 louvers in the hood and side panels.

Vince Burgos' roadster appeared in my book *Hot Rods & Customs of the 1960s.* Changed and updated in the '70s, here is this beautiful '29 Ford again.

New items include a 292-ci Chevy engine with single AFB carburetor. A Walker radiator replaced the original. The stick shift came out, and a Powerglide transmission took its place.

The front end still has a dropped axle, but coil pads and Volvo springs replaced the leaf springs. He also went to coil springs in the rear. Bill Clenendon did the black, pleated Naugahyde upholstery and black top. Where there was formerly a trunk, there is now a rumble seat. Chromed Buick wire wheels are now his choice. Burgos repainted the roadster '65 Mustang maroon with black fenders. Standing by the roadster with Vince is his wife, Rose. This photo was taken August 27, 1972. Vince and Rose still have the roadster.

In September 1972, I ventured to Andy Brizio's shop in South San Francisco. It being a Saturday, the usual routine was for many rodders to gather there.

Among them was Mike Haas, driving his newly created *Odyssey*, a fiberglass '23 T that was part roadster and part spacecraft. Haas grafted a '71 Corvette rear top section into the back of the roadster body, producing a rear window. The custom nosepiece was made of fiberglass, and the chopped T radiator shell was aluminum. Pete Ogden engineered the Odyssey and was involved with various parts of its construction. The chassis was built by Tony Cotta.

Front wheels are Ogden-modified 18x3.30 Kellerman wires with Airheart disc brakes. Haas painted a multicolored blending of different hues on each side of the body.

The *Odyssey* was powered by a 1964 Corvette with dual AFB carburetors and an Iskenderian cam. It also featured Andy's *Instant T*-style headers. The transmission is a modified Turbo 400 automatic, mated to a '64 Chevy rear end. Transverse leaf springs were used.

Wishbone axles are the chromed hairpin type. The rear wheels are 12-inch wide E.T. mags wrapped with Firestone tires. The color hues on the left side are pearl blue, while the right side is pearl orange, with space-age graphics adorning the front, sides, and rear.

Ken Foster of A Action Interiors fashioned the brown-and-orange Naugahyde upholstery with custom seats and brown carpet. The steering unit comes from a '56 Ford, and the deep-dish steering wheel was made by Covico. The taillights are from a Barracuda, installed upside down.

This photo of the *Odyssey* was taken at the Visalia Roadster Roundup in September 1972.

This '23 Ford touring in the striking light-blue paint scheme with lavender trim, owned by Paul Lohrey, won the "Rodders Choice" award at the '72 Roadster Roundup in Visalia, California.

The complementary two-tone blue interior is done in pleated Naugahyde. Stewart Warner instruments are in the dash, and the steering wheel is stock T. The headlamp structures are original with sealed-beams inside.

A small-block Chevy is crammed under the hood. It's stock except for homemade headers that are chromed. The original T spark lever does the shifting through a Chevy Turbo 400 series transmission. Independent rear suspension and the disc brake assembly is courtesy of Corvette. The front suspension was homemade, with Camaro discs and refitted spindles; the rack-and-pinion steering is from an MG.

This '29 Ford roadster, built on a '32 Ford frame, was originally an early-1950s Barris Kustom, but Bruce Bell of San Mateo, California, refurbished it in the 1970s. (Notice Barris' crest on side of cowl.)

Bell chopped 4 inches from the windshield, molded-in the cowl, filled the '32 grille shell, and removed the doors and trunk handles. Bruce made the point, "done in lead and not plastic."

The roadster was painted jet-black lacquer with complementary tan Naugahyde upholstery.

Suspension goodies include a chromed, tube-style, dropped front axle, Volvo tube shocks, and hairpin-style tubular radius rods. Dietz 820 headlights and 16-inch Kelsey-Hayes wheels are part of the appearance package.

The 286-ci Ford flathead uses Jahns pistons, Grant rings, and an Engle cam. The heads are Edelbrock, the manifold is Edmunds, and the carbs are Stromberg 97s. A '39 Ford transmission is tied to the rear end, from a '35 Ford with 4.11 gears.

Mel Swanson calls this 1928 Ford roadster his High School Sweetheart. You could say he's fond of a 327-ci Chevy, with an Iskenderian cam kit, 11.5:1 compression pistons, an M/T offset intake manifold, two four-barrel carbs, and chromed Hedman exhaust headers. A stick-shift transmission connects to a '50 Oldsmobile rear end, mounted with dual-pivot radius rods. The '28 Ford frame is completely boxed. Tube shocks are used on all four corners.

Seats, door panels, kick panels, and the rumble seat are pleated black Naugahyde. Light brown was Swanson's choice for the body, with dark brown used on the fenders and trim. Firestone tires are on Buick wire wheels.

These two Chevy customs were photographed October 1,1972, at the second of Rod Powell's annual picnics in Salinas, California.

The black '56 Chevy sedan delivery was chopped by Mario Sanchez of Hollister, California, and owned by Rocky DeMateo of Salinas. The paint work, including the murals on the sides, was the work of Rod Powell.

The yellow '55 Chevy, owned by Bill DeWitt of Hollister, started out as a two-door Nomad station wagon. Willie Wilde and Butch Hurlhey, working in Powell's shop, chopped 4 1/2 inches from the top. The engine, lifted from a '69 Camaro Z-28, turned the wheels through a Muncie four-speed transmission. The black Naugahyde upholstery was produced by Monte's of Salinas. The great paint was candy-yellow pearl with tangerine flames, with Powell again controlling the paint gun.

Another outstanding car at the 1972 Powell picnic was Jerry Nielsen's 283-powered 1958 Corvette.

Ted Mitchell of Salinas provided the customizing touches: de-chroming all the emblems, removing door handles and installing electric openers, and slightly flaring the fender wells. He also installed frenched 1960 Buick dual headlights.

Rod Powell worked his paint gun magic, applying candy tangerine over pearl. The cove-area flames were done with gold leaf. Andy Southard pinstriped the edges in white. The roof was candied in gold with 3/4-inch ghost stripes.

Black Naugahyde with buttons was the choice for interior fabric, and the tires were Goodyear Polyglas, mounted on aluminum mag wheels.

This is not your run-of-the-mill '72 Chevy Cheyenne pickup truck. Owner Jerry Nielsen of Gilroy, California, in the light-colored jacket, wanted something different, and certainly got what he wanted. The custom mechanical work was put in the hands of Ron Covell of Campbell, California. In the process of installing a '70 Jaguar rear end with 3.23 gears, Covell made custom cross-members and special mounts, extended the hubs 2 inches, shortened the drive shaft, and installed Heim joints at all suspension points. The work retains the Jaguar inboard disc brakes and dual coil-overs.

Wilhelm Custom Shop in San Jose stepped the A-frames for a total drop of 4 inches. The truck rides on Koni shocks, with wire wheels from a '54 Buick Skylark and Goodyear Polyglas GT tires.

The grille was a custom fabrication. Rod Powell applied the forest-green paint, flamed in lime pearl, and pinstriped in gold. . . . Joe the Chromer was responsible for the plating.

I took this picture of a '40 Mercury four-door sedan, because I like '40 Mercs and currently own one. The location was the Cow Palace Car Show in South San Francisco. The show dates were November 17-19, 1972.

John Moses of Mountain View, California, was the owner of this stock-appearing sedan. Here are some of the customizing touches Moses added. He removed the chrome pieces on the front of the hood, removed the trunk handle and smoothed off the trunk, and mounted a '49 Chevy license-plate bracket to the bumper. The taillights remained stock.

Oldsmobile power was under the hood. The interior was pearl-white Naugahyde, and the window moldings were chromed. The wheels were also chromed and baldy hubcaps were fitted. Around the stock speedometer panel, the dash held four Stewart Warner gauges. The rear quarter window had a "For Sale" sign; I wonder if it sold.

Starbird Customs of Mulvane, Kansas, created the *Love American Style* Machine in the late 1960s, using a '37 Ford coupe. It was on display at the Cow Palace Car Show in November 1972 when I took this photo.

Earlier in 1972, the car had been restyled for Gary Enslinger of Wichita. Originally the coupe was sectioned 6 inches, fenders and running boards were customized, and the hood was extended 10 inches.

The grille cavity was also extended and reformed using polished aluminum for the grille and locating the headlights there.

During the recustomizing, the back of the coupe became a panel truck. All of this work was done in sheet metal. The windshield and front of the car had an electric lift top. It was painted pearl white, with candy-red stripes and stars, with the plush diamond-tufted red-velvet and pearl-white Naugahyde interior creating a dramatic effect.

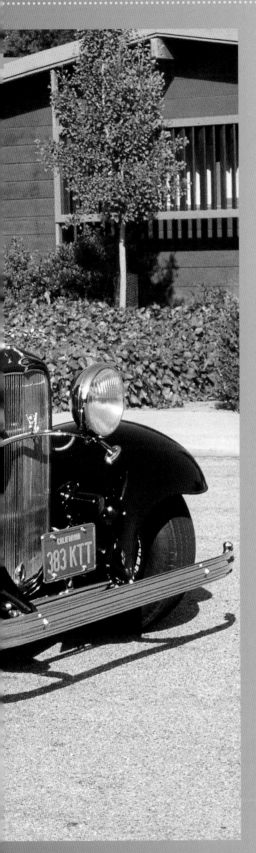

# Chapter
# 2 1973-1974

If you had a driver's license in 1973, you remember the ramifications of the fuel shortage that stunned the motorized public that year. Gasoline prices that had been in the 30-cents-per-gallon range soared to double and triple that amount in some areas of the country. Long lines formed at gas stations. Purchases were made on even or odd days, depending on your license plate number. Tempers were quick to explode. Fuel-thirsty cars were out of favor, and a national speed limit of 55 mph was imposed.

A replay of the 1950s was playing well with a TV show called *Happy Days*, a movie called *American Graffiti*, and a Broadway musical called *Grease*. Each one cast a favorable light on the car culture and youth.

Other television hits included *M*A*S*H*, *All in the Family*, and *The Waltons*. They were big, but not big like the Sears Tower in Chicago, which was completed in 1973 and stood 1,454 feet tall.

Hot pants and leisure suits were popular attire for women and men respectively. Mood rings, lava lamps, shag carpets, and water beds were all part of the diversion. For the most daring of pranksters, streaking—running naked at public events—was the newest form of freedom of expression.

Disco and funk were moving into the musical mainstream reviving the career of the Bee Gees, but cranked-up rock 'n' roll was still powerful, with the likes of Led Zeppelin and the Rolling Stones. In 1973 a plane crash took the life of singer Jim Croce, and Bobby Darrin died after a heart operation.

The emerald-green pinstriping on this '32 Ford roadster is some of my handiwork. That's $40 worth of striping you're looking at! The job included striping the side-panel louvers and placing double lines around lime-green body moldings. The roadster body was painted a '72 GMC dark-green metallic color with black fenders. Ken Foster of Sacramento did the saddle-tan Naugahyde.

Les Owen, a member of the San Jose Roadster Club, was the owner. His rod won the "People's Choice" award at the Pismo Beach roadster roundup.

Under the skin, Owen had a 302-ci '70 Ford Mustang engine with a Joe Hunt magneto. The front suspension was built by Les Erben with an assist from his nephew Duke DePonzi. A '68 Jaguar XKE donated the rear end and the steering unit. A Pinto flex shaft was instrumental in adapting the steering unit.

My photographs of this roadster were published in the May 1976 issue of *Street Rodder* magazine.

In 1973 a new era began, with the advent of the wildly styled and customized pickup trucks. One of the wildest ever was this 1973 Chevy step-side pickup owned by 26-year-old Mike Farley of San Mateo.

Back then, money went a long way, so with $6,500 you could buy a pickup and build something the way Mike did. The engine was a stock 350-ci Chevy with an Accel ignition, an Andy Brizio manifold, a 471 GMC blower, and a Holley carburetor.

A 10-inch wide fiberglass scoop was molded into the hood so the blower and carb would have clearance. The transmission was a Turbo-Hydra-matic and the running gear was stock. Goodyear Polyglas tires rode on polished aluminum wheels.

At America's auto racing mecca in Indiana, Mark Donohue (1973) and Gordon Johncock (1974) each won an Indy 500 championship. The Miami Dolphins put together back-to-back Super Bowl victories, while the Oakland As grabbed the World Series for three years in a row (1972-74).

The "Sam Barris" award at the 1973 Sacramento Autorama went to Bill Roach for his highly customized '40 Ford Tudor sedan. And in keeping with the ongoing popularity of Model Ts, Chuck Corsello took top honors at the '73 Oakland Roadster Show with his '23 Ford roadster. Corsello's T featured a beer keg gas tank, Jaguar rear end, psychedelic paint, and a fuel-injected Corvette engine. The 1974 "America's Most Beautiful Roadster" award at the Oakland Roadster Show went to Jim Vasser with his black, fiberglass-bodied '23 Ford touring, with brown steel fenders and chromed wire wheels.

Mike Farley decided to "accessorize" his Stepside in this photo with pretty Kathleen "Cookie" Urbina, from Daly City, California. Good call, Mike!

"Keep On Truckin'," a popular saying with everybody who owned a truck in the early 1970s, was painted in gold-leaf lettering on the back of Farley's Chevy cab. The overall paint scheme, guaranteed to catch people's attention, consisted of black, pearl white, candy red, and blue, with blue pinstriping. M & M made the tarp with the Mr. Natural "Truckin" character that covered the truck bed. Custom taillights were '70 Ford Mustang, inserted vertically.

Inside the cab, black-and-white Naugahyde was the choice for the upholstery by M & M Custom of San Bruno—including top inserts in the cab and pinstriping. Other interesting features were the wooden steering wheel by Grant, and a Dixco tachometer mounted on the steering column.

When I photographed Ray Callejo's 1915 Ford C-cab in 1973, I took 180 pictures. I've been told I overshoot pictures, but with lovely model Lolita Rio, a *Garden of Eden* nightclub entertainer from San Francisco, I couldn't resist!

Callejo, who designed his C-cab from a miniature plastic model, made the frame from custom-made square tubing with all the welds filled and smoothed. The front end has a chromed tube axle; a '54 Chevy donated the brakes, and a '65 Chevy provided the rear end and coil springs.

When it came to power, he went big, with a 427-ci Chevy engine. The extras include a 671 GMC blower with dual AFB carbs, Jahns pistons, Howard rods, Engle cam, and Joe Hunt magneto. The transmission is a B & M Hydra-matic.

Steve Archer built the body from waterproof plywood, then fiberglassed over it. The color scheme is black with blue fenders. Averill of Fresno added blue pinstriping. Sealed-beam headlights were inserted into the original T-style headlight fixtures, and wide-pleated brown Naugahyde upholstery by Bob Epperson can be found inside.

This Regency red '32 Ford cabriolet is owned by Ray and Jo Milazzo. Ray and Jo and I go back a long time together. He's a fellow New Yorker, and his '56 Ford was featured in my first book, *Custom Cars of the 1950s*.

His cabriolet has a chopped top, a rolled rear pan with bobbed rear fenders, '66 Catalina taillights, and custom front and rear nerf bars.

A 283-ci-Chevy provides the power, which is transferred to Goodyear Wide Tread GT tires via a Powerglide transmission and a '56 Chevy rear end. The Goodyear rubber is mounted on Dayton wire wheels. Chuck's Auto Body gets credit for the paint, and Dennis Drake was the upholstery guy who completed the tan Naugahyde interior.

One thing I liked about going to the L.A. Roadster Show and Swap Meet was seeing some of the vehicles parked outside the show area.

One pickup that caught my attention was Ray Bartnick's '53 Ford. He called the truck the *Praying Mantis*. According to Ray, the name came from a near accident when all he could do was grab the wheel and pray!

Some of the particulars of this truck include a small-block Ford with Cruise-o-Matic, a chromed 2 1/2-inch dropped axle, and chromed wheels with baldy hubcaps. The tailgate is paneled with 1/8-inch steel sheeting, and '71 Ford Pinto taillights are mounted in a flat panel below the tailgate. Did you notice the "Keep On Truckin'" license plate frame?

The running boards are black lacquer with two Model T step plates. Inside, the upholstery and dash are jet black. All the paint, pinstriping, and artwork was handled by Walt Prey of Van Nuys, California.

How about this '36 Dodge sedan delivery? You don't see many of these, especially this "humpback" model. Owners Bob and JoAnn Jeffords Jr. of Paradise, California, brought this truck to Lodi, California, for the 1973 West Coast Street Rod Mini Nationals.

Bob chopped the top 3 1/2 inches, added the diamond-shape side windows, and painted it the wild pearl-lavender and plum colors. The matching pearl-lavender-and-white Naugahyde interior was the work of Luckinbills of Chico.

This delivery was assisted by a '70 Ford 351-ci Cleveland engine with a 725-cfm Holley carburetor, Mallory dual-point ignition, and custom-built exhaust headers. A Ford four-speed with a Hurst shifter was linked to a '70 Ford Mach I rear end.

On Sunday, June 17, 1973, at the L.A. Roadster Club Car Show and Swap Meet, I was thrilled to see Dick Smith's '32 Ford roadster. I had seen it previously at a car show in Phoenix, Arizona.

Smith, of Phoenix, Arizona, acquired this '32 Ford roadster in 1949. As he built it into a rod, he installed a chromed dropped axle and split wishbones, made the headlight bar and the stainless steel grille bars, and chopped the windshield. Additional body work consisted of shaving the door handles, filling the grille shell, and notching the solid side panels to clear the engine valve covers. The black lacquer paint job was Smith's own.

A '51 Chrysler 354-ci engine with a Winfield cam, Challenger intake manifold, and a four-barrel carburetor can show some muscle. The exhaust headers were hand made. A side shift Packard transmission mated to a '40 Ford rear end with 3.54 gears gets the ponies to the pavement. Dick stitched his own black-and-white Naugahyde upholstery. He completed the job in only five years.

After Smith owned the roadster for 40 years, he sold it; now it can be seen at the Henry Ford Museum in Dearborn, Michigan. It's preserved!

The gold pinstriping looks good on the Rickeys' jet-black 1973 Chevy Cheyenne Super/10 pickup. Jack lowered the truck by cutting the front coil springs and de-arching the rear elliptic springs.

The 8-inch-wide front wheels and 10-inch-wide rears were chromed and fitted with Concorde G-600 belted tires. Custom-chromed side pipes were also part of the custom treatment.

The grille centers were blacked out to give a tube-grille effect. Rear fenders house '70 Mustang taillights. The engine and running gear were completely stock. This photo shows Jack and Marilyn in 1973. They were members of the California Stepsides Club.

I knew Jack and Marilyn Rickey for many years, and striped many cars and trucks for them before they asked me to do their new 1973 Chevy Cheyenne truck.

It was a moderate job: hood, sides, rear fenders, fender wells, tailgate, and around the taillights. Their truck was so nice, two months later I photographed it for a magazine article, which appeared in the *Rod Action Yearbook* in 1975.

After all these years, I can still pick up my brush and do pinstriping.

David Mathison drove his cranberry-red 1935 Ford roadster to the Mini Nationals from Bremerton, Washington.

In 1969 his roadster won the "Best Open" award at the Old Timer's Rod Run in Tacoma, Washington. Before he could really celebrate that prize, the car was demolished in an accident. My picture shows its reincarnation, after the roadster underwent four years of work being put back together.

Custom work includes a chopped windshield, white Carson-style padded top, and pleated, pearl-white Naugahyde upholstery. The cowl air vent is smoothed over, and the doors and rumble-seat handles were removed. The gauges and dash are '40 Ford.

A '50 Oldsmobile 303-ci engine with a '53 Olds manifold and a '56 Cadillac quad carburetor provide a hot setup. Cooling things down is a cut-down '60 Ford Thunderbird radiator. The transmission, including floor shift, is from a '39 Ford and the gears are the 26-tooth Zephyr set. Components from a '48 Merc make up the suspension all around.

The Lodi Mini Nationals of 1973 was also the site where John Corno's beautiful '32 Ford Victoria was photographed.

My friend Al Drake told me this car was built in Los Angeles by the late Mike Thelen of Buffalo Motors. The engine was a 289-ci Ford with an automatic transmission and a Ford rear end. The paint is Cadillac firemist brown acrylic lacquer, highlighted with orange-and-gold pinstriping.

Brown Naugahyde, with buttons and tufted, was the choice for upholstery, and the top had a padded, brown Naugahyde insert. Chrome Zenith wire wheels were used all around, with deep-dished versions on the rear.

Touring cars were popular at the '73 Lodi Mini Nationals, but this outstanding '28 Ford touring was exceptional! Owner Bill Mendoza was building a roadster pickup, when he located this touring body and decided to make a swap.

Mendoza's friend Mickey Meredith painted it with a red acrylic enamel used on '69 Dodge Chargers. Neil Averill did the subtle gold pinstriping. Ken Foster of A Action Interiors in Sacramento did the dark-brown Naugahyde upholstery, the pockets sewn into all four doors, and the black all-weather top.

The 289-ci engine from a '67 Mustang has the Shelby dress-up accessories. It also has a 750-cfm Holley carb sitting on an Edelbrock manifold, plus exhaust headers by Hedman. The transmission is a Ford C-4 automatic. Les Erben of Components Ltd., in San Jose installed the '64 Jaguar front and rear independent suspension components, along with Jaguar rack-and-pinion steering. Chromed running boards and wheels give an added sparkle.

Ever have a case of seller's remorse? Owner Guy Osborn of Coburg, Oregon, built this '29 Ford pickup in 1955, sold it, then bought it back again.

Up front is a 3 1/2-inch dropped Bell axle. A '40 Willys donated the steering unit. Chrysler wire wheels are mounted with Goodyear tires—4.25s in front, 8.20s at the rear. Ken Higgins of Eugene, Oregon, did the green Naugahyde button-tuft upholstery. Wayne Loesch, who gets credit for the Verdoro green-and-black lacquer paint, owned the pickup for a while. In 1967, he replaced the Ford flathead with a 327-ci Chevy. The transmission remained a '39 Ford, with Zephyr gears, going to a Ford rear end.

Between Guy and Wayne showing the pickup, it won a total of 67 trophies. Guy passed away in 1995.

This three-quarter rear view of Roach's '40 sedan shows fenders molded to the body, louvers on the hood, and the sunken antenna on the rear side of the front fender. Other notable custom features included the license plate bracket molded to the trunk and the rolled panel beneath the rear of the body. Nerf bars act as exhaust pipes. Fitting nicely into the fender contours are '41 Studebaker taillights.

Art Himsl and Mike Haas did the candy-apple red, acrylic lacquer paint, with Art also handling the pinstriping. Kenny Foster did the narrow-pleated, pearl-white Naugahyde upholstery with black floor carpets.

Bill's father, Dale Roach, rebuilt the dash panel, using Stewart Warner gauges behind a smoke plastic cover. A '72 Ford Torino power/tilt steering column with a Shelby steering wheel got a lot of attention as well. Fourteen-inch Ford spoked wheels are wrapped with Goodyear Polyglas tires.

This classic sedan still exists today, and is owned by Dick Falk of Concord, California.

At the Lodi Mini Nationals, June 30, 1973, I saw this super show car, an old-timer resurrected by Bill Roach of Concord, California.

When Dave Cunningham bought this '40 Ford Tudor sedan, it had been channeled over the frame, sectioned, and lowered by the original owner. Cunningham wanted to take it further, so Barris Kustoms got involved. Canted, quad headlights from a '57 Lincoln were tunneled in the front fenders. Then the front and rear fender openings were enlarged and flared, and the added touch of Pontiac nerf bars front and rear was mixed in.

The drivetrain consists of a 302-ci Ford V-8, backed by a C-4 automatic transmission, plugged into a Mustang rear end. The front axle is a '40 Ford, dropped 2 inches, and the brakes are Mustang discs.

In the early 1970s, Bill Roach restored the sedan. He had Dennis Craig, Pete Ogden, Bob Burton, Dick Falk, Ed Fry, and Kenny Foster all working on it to get the car ready for the '73 Street Rod Nationals in Tulsa, Oklahoma.

**H**arry Westergard was one of the true legends of custom car building. He created his version of this '39 Ford convertible in 1945. When I photographed it in August 1973, the car was owned by Mickey Sanders of Watsonville, California, who told me some of the car's history.

Westergard chopped the top 3 1/2 inches, then made a removable hardtop from a '40 Chevy coupe. Stock convertible clamps secure the front, while footlocker-type clamps secure the rear.

The car has a very clean and flowing appearance, due to some fine details. For instance, the complete trunk lid was molded in, and all the fenders were molded to the body. The rear license plate was artfully recessed into the trunk. Westergard saw no reason to replace the stock taillights. You may recognize the impressive grille as being from a Packard. The headlights were frenched, but they have a stock '40 Ford look. Pleated white Naugahyde was used in the interior.

One of the early Oldsmobile overhead-valve V-8s was selected for supplying the power to a '41 Cadillac transmission and a narrowed '48 Cadillac rear end.

**A**nother Barris Kustom was this '40 Ford coupe, with a chopped top and a channeled body. The paint is pearl white with free-form lavender scallops. It was an early custom, dating to the late 1940s, and owned by Tom Hocker.

In the process of chopping the top, 2 1/2 inches were sliced from the front and 3 1/2 inches from the rear. The windshield was raked, with the center post removed and glass V-butted together. In typical Barris fashion, the drip moldings were removed.

The front axle was dropped and the driveshaft tunnel was raised. All the fenders were molded to the body. The DeLuxe grille sides were filled, the door handles were removed, and the dual headlights were frenched.

A Cadillac supplied the engine and a '49 Pontiac provided the front and rear bumpers. When I took this picture, the car belonged to Ralph Garcia, who has since passed away.

Ron Courtney of McMinnville, Oregon, originally built this '51 Ford club coupe in the mid-1950s. Courtney, an expert body man, took out a 5-inch horizontal section all around the body, and fabricated the grille from tubing and sheet metal. The rear fins were built from sheet metal stock, affixed to the quarter panels, and fiberglassed. Custom taillights were set into the fins, and the rear deck lid was rebuilt. In shaping the rear body panels, Courtney made them quite similar to the front of the car.

John Corno rejuvenated this old-time custom in the 1970s. During the refurbishing process, the original upholsterer, Stan Jones, created the red-and-white Naugahyde. Gary Crisp and Harold Walton did body work and applied the fiesta-red paint. Dave Kane installed a Ford 351-ci Cleveland engine. Dave Dohenick and Vern White rebuilt the running gear and suspension. Trim and bumper parts were fabricated by Gilbertson Machine Shop.

Winning the "America's Most Beautiful Roadster" title in 1971 may have provided a little incentive for Lonnie Gilbertson. He and his '23 T fiberglass roadster pickup returned in 1974. Of course, there were some changes made between those two dates.

Let's begin with the hand-made independent front suspension, '71 Toyota Mark II spindles, disc brakes, and Spax adjustable shocks. Under the hood is a 327-ci '68 Chevy, Mallory dual-point distributor, 471 GMC supercharger, and a 750 double-pumper carburetor. A '63 Plymouth Torque-Flite transmission, with a B & M adapter, is hooked into a '65 Plymouth torque converter. The rear end is from a '66 Jaguar.

An aluminum hood (lying on the floor) was hand made and contoured to fit the supercharger. The grille shell was lengthened 1 inch to cover the custom radiator, which had a 3-inch core. Goodrich tires were mounted on wire wheels.

Gary Crisp gets credit for the pearl-yellow paint with a sunrise scene on the driver side and sunset view on the passenger side.

Here's a nice custom '52 Ford pickup, shown at the January 1974 San Jose Autorama. Sonny Siebert of San Jose, the owner and builder, did his own work from the Blossom Hill Auto Body Shop. His truck had a tremendous amount of customizing.

The top was chopped 3 1/2 inches, the body was sectioned 5 inches, and the hood was sectioned as well. The body was channeled 5 inches over the frame. A '57 Corvette gave up its grille and a Lincoln forfeited its headlights, which were subsequently frenched. The hood has 74 louvers with an air scoop up front. For maximizing the visual impact, the running boards were chromed and the exhaust stacks were run up along the cab. Candy-red paint with flames in a darker shade of red combine for red-hot looks, with pleated tan Naugahyde for the interior.

The horses were provided by a 302-ci Ford with a Crane cam, TRW pistons, a Holley 715 carburetor, and a Mallory ignition. A Ford C-4 automatic transmission delivered the power to a '67 Ford pickup rear end.

The jet-black paint on this customized '54 Chevy pickup led to the name *Black Jack.* Viewed from the front, this truck displays many of the customizer's favorite tricks— tunneled and frenched triple headlights, double Studebaker pans, and a grille that combines chromed bars and bullets. The hood has been reworked with an air scoop in front.

*Black Jack* was lowered, had its door handles removed, and wears a chopped top. Firestone tires were mounted on chromed wire wheels, and the running boards were also chromed and made use of step plates. Continental Plating did all the chrome. The black Naugahyde upholstery was stitched by Gary and Danny.

A Naugahyde tarp covers the bed, and you'll find double Studebaker pans molded underneath the tailgate, with a 3-inch chromed bar running the full length of the pans. The taillights are '59 Cadillac bullet style.

The owner was Paul McElley of Hayward, California.

**P**eople ask me, "How many pictures do you take when covering a rod or custom being built?" I tell them, "It's a lot!"

For example, I started shooting Tom Prufer's '23 T when construction began at Ron Covell's shop in Campbell, California. From March 24 to September 16, 1973, I took 96 pictures.

Then from November 28 to December 15, 1973, the roadster was at Rod Powell's shop in Salinas. Rod painted the car black, then masked off the flame pattern and painted it.

Rod was busy, and to save time, he asked if I would pinstripe the flamed edges for him. The photos of the painting process, including my pinstriping, came to a total of 120 pictures.

Finally there were pictures taken of the road test for *Hot Rod/Rod & Custom* magazine. Between January 20 and February 6, 1974, I shot another 120 photos. That's a grand total of 336 pictures, or 28 rolls of film.

**R**od & Custom magazine artist Tom Daniel drew a track T roadster in 1972 that was out of sight.

When Tom Prufer of Los Gatos, California, saw the drawing in 1973, he looked at the drawing every day for a month, then decided he was going to build that '23 Ford roadster.

Prufer and Ron Covell of Campbell, a master of aluminum and steel work, brought the roadster to life. The frame was built with a 104-inch wheelbase, a '32 Ford dropped axle, split wishbones, friction-type shocks, and drum brakes from a modernized '40 Ford.

The body and turtledeck were built out of fiberglass by Steve Archer. Covell made the aluminum nose piece, hood, full belly pan with louvers, and chrome outside headers, putting a total of 75 louvers in the hood and side panels. Pete Ogden made the tube grille, nerf bars, and aluminum gas tank.

A 155-ci '73 Capri V-6 engine and four-speed Capri transmission was used. Jim Babb built the brass radiator. The rear end is a substantially modified '72 Datsun 510 independent assembly. Firestone tires were chosen to be mounted on Zenith wire wheels. Ken Foster did the upholstery in antique mahogany Naugahyde, with dark-brown rugs. This photo was taken January 20, 1974.

What do you see when you look at this beautiful custom '55 Ford Victoria? How about '59 Chevy quad headlights that are canted and frenched? And how about a '54 Chevy grille that has been shortened and given a few extra teeth?

Bill Hines was the body and paint man on this project for owner Wally Marquez of South Gate, California. The Victoria's body was lowered by reworking the A-frames, C-ing the frame, and de-arching the springs. Hines had to enlarge the grille opening to accomplish his grille-customizing task. He also rounded the corners on the hood and trunk lid, and de-chromed the hood. Handles were removed from the electrically operated doors. The taillights from a '56 Mercury station wagon were frenched.

Lakes pipes protrude from the custom-built housing, which was flared and frenched into the front half of the rocker panel. A 272-ci Ford engine got things cranking. Ed Martinez did the all-black, pleated Naugahyde upholstery. The paint was called candy-turquoise lacquer.

This photo was taken at the March 1974 Winternationals Car Show at the Los Angeles Convention Center.

Another fine customized pickup belonged to Dave Bethel of Salinas, California. This 1970 Chevy, C10 pickup, has a stock 292-ci six-cylinder engine for economy.

The first go-around for customizing Dave Bethel's Chevy pickup was at Rod Powell's Custom Shop in the early 1970s. There was some mild body "cleanup" work, but the main focus was the white acrylic enamel paint highlighted by multicolored ribbons—a popular cosmetic of that era. Rod painted the hood, body sides, rear fenders, and tailgate. Pastel colors of gold, light yellow, blue, and red were used for the ribbons, with their edges pinstriped in black.

Additional custom items added at that time were Road Hugger belted tires on ten-inch Ansen mags, chromed side pipes, and a black Naugahyde tonneau cover over the bed. Bethel also opted for the wide-pleated Naugahyde interior by Monte Custom Upholstery of Salinas.

On the second customizing go-around, again at Powell's shop, Willie Wilde performed a 4-inch "Chop Top" operation. The work was done with care, so only the area being chopped required repainting. The lovely model in this April 1974 picture is Sherrill Bethel.

America's Most Beautiful Roadster at the 1974 Oakland Roadster Show was this 1914 Ford T called *California Touring*. That's Jim Vasser of San Jose, standing with his trophy winner, which took more than one year to construct. (Check out the flared pants.)

Usually there are many people to credit for a successful project. In this case, Denny Craig did a lot of the fabrication; Steve Archer did the fiberglass body; Ken Foster did the brown Naugahyde upholstery; Jim Babb did the grand brass radiator; and Joe the Chromer did the brightwork.

California Touring has a 112-inch wheelbase, a Bell front axle, Airheart Disc brakes, and Corvair steering. Andy's Instant T supplied the chassis. The body is black with brown steel fenders.

The '67 Chevy 350 powerplant has an array of goodies, including a high-performance cam, Hedman headers, a 400 Turbo-Hydra-matic with B & M shifter, a Hayden transmission cooler, and a 471 GMC blower, modified for street use by Andy Brizio.

Do you remember what the Lone Ranger's horse's name was? It wasn't Blackie. The masked man named his horse Silver. Not a bad color for a '29 Ford roadster, either. This all-steel body sits on a '32 Ford frame, with some nice features, such as a chromed dropped axle, chromed tube shocks and springs, and a Teflon-bushed system for a smoother, quieter ride. The steering unit is from a '56 Ford pickup, while spindles and brakes are '40 Ford. The classic three-piece hood, with 114 louvers on the side panels, was crafted by Jack Heggemann.

L.A. Roadster Club member Bob Chrisman of Simi, California, owned this car when I photographed it at the Ninth Annual Bay Area Roadster/L.A. Roadster Clubs Meet at Pismo Beach, California, in 1974.

Chrisman's choice of power was a 350-ci '74 Chevy with Edelbrock manifold and Holley four-barrel carb. A Muncie four-speed is hooked up to an early Thunderbird rear end with Jaguar coil-over-shocks suspension. Although the black Naugahyde upholstery and pinstriping complement the silver lacquer paint, not long after this picture was taken, this roadster was painted chrome yellow and reupholstered in brown grained Naugahyde.

Tom Myre of Union Lake, Michigan, was the owner of this radical '35 Ford three-window coupe he called *Crown Coupe*. Myre recustomized this old championship car, formerly owned and built by Mervin Colver of Des Plaines, Illinois. When Colver owned the car, it was known as *Little Beaver*. Colver was responsible for the 4-inch chopped top and the 4-inch body-section job. He also built the Z-frame and channeled the body. All the running gear was chromed.

This photo was taken in 1974 at a rod and customs show at the Anaheim Convention Center. The show was sponsored by Pickups Ltd., a Southern California car club.

Myre's *Crown Coupe* originally had '39 Chevy headlight buckets, with Lucas lights molded on top of fenders. When it was recustomized, the lights were set inside a front panel with a movable grille work over lights. The nose piece is a chrome Edsel grille.

Other changes include a Landau-style top covering over the rear portion of the roof. The original running boards became all metal and were molded, with a taper, to inside the rear fender; the rear fender wells were opened and radiused; and the Metalflake blue paint was changed to pearl white with subtle black pinstriping.

The interior has a custom-made dash with nine Stewart Warner gauges. The bucket seats are from a '57 Corvette and are covered in pearl-white Naugahyde. The original '59 Cadillac taillight lenses were changed to taillights in the simulated recessed bumper. Under the hood is a Chevy with four carbs and lots of chrome.

I really like the candy-red, silver, and wildly flamed Metalflake paint job on this '39 Ford coupe, owned by Pete Fergerson of Tarzana, California. Zipper's custom painting gets the credit. The black, pleated Naugahyde interior—including the package tray—was done by Jerry's Auto Upholstery.

Other notable details include '40 Ford headlight rims; '41 Studebaker taillights fit into the contour of rear fenders; chromed front and rear nerf bars; and outside-type headers running along under the body and turning out in front of the rear wheels.

**A**nd now for something completely different, how about a mid-engined Dodge A-100 van pickup? Tom McMullen, owner and customizer, chopped the top, filled in the rear quarter windows, and did most of the body work himself.

Under the tonneau cover is a 454-ci Chevy with a 671 blower. Transmission is a Turbo-Hydra-matic with a very short driveshaft mated to a '58 Oldsmobile rear end that was cut down by 10 inches. Summers Brothers supplied the axles.

The rear wheel wells were moved back 7 inches and widened 3 inches. Goodyear tires are mounted on Cragar S/S mags up front and on Supertrick wheels on the rear. A tube axle is used up front with Ford spindles and Airheart disc brakes.

**T**his photo of Rasmussen's '41 Ford was taken at the 1975 Oakland Roadster Show.

An extremely sharp rod and custom enthusiast will recognize that the front fenders are from a '48 Ford, the grille is cut down from a '54 Chevy, the parking lights are from a Chrysler, headlights are frenched, and the ripple bumpers are from a '49 Plymouth.

The interior is black Naugahyde with square patterns, covering reclining, bucket-type front seats from a Datsun. The steering box is stock '41 Ford, but the tilt steering column is from a '67 Buick. The wide whitewalls are on chromed reversed wheels with bullet hubcaps.

Under the hood is a 327-ci '65 Chevy, backed by a '65 Chevy Powerglide, and hooked into a '64 Chevy Nova rear end. The front brakes are '41 Ford; the rears are '64 Nova. Rasmussen was affiliated with the Early Wheels Car Club of San Jose.

On Saturday, December 7, 1974, I stopped at Vintage Ford Center in Santa Clara, California. I always liked to drive by to see what was for sale.

One of the cars for sale was this '39 Ford Tudor sedan with a '40 Ford DeLuxe front end. Bob Kennedy originally built the car; Bob Dodge chopped the top. The '40 Ford-style headlights were frenched. The Ford bumpers were replaced with custom-made chrome nerf bars. The door and trunk handles were removed, and '41 Studebaker taillights, placed vertically, fit the rear fender contour.

The sedan was painted purple, with a light flake; the flames are a combination of red and yellow-gold. The upholstery was black-and-chartreuse Naugahyde.

Under the hood was a '51 Oldsmobile with an Iskenderian roller cam and four Stromberg carburetors. The transmission was Cadillac/LaSalle, and the rear end was Oldsmobile with coil springs.

This chopped and channeled '41 Ford club coupe is painted cherry black—a combination of black base, pearl, burgundy, and clear lacquer. It was the choice of owner George Rasmussen, the man behind the wheel, who posed for this picture with his pretty wife, Anita.

I know a little history on this car. Don Reid of Salinas, who previously owned it, obtained it from a soldier stationed at Fort Ord. It was already chopped and channeled and had the fade-away fenders.

Don had some work done by Valley Customs in Burbank, including a dark metallic maroon paint job. A dropped axle was installed up front and a C-frame in the rear. In 1953, Don entered the coupe in the Third Annual Oakland Roadster Show.

# Chapter

# 3

# *1975-1976*

During the middle years of the 1970s, few things fell outside the scope of the buildup to and the celebration of America's bicentennial. It was a momentous occasion in American history: A Fourth of July spectacular and all-out exhibition of pride that could only be compared to those that took place at the end of World Wars I and II. The usual parades, fireworks, and reenactments of historic events became bigger and better and more meaningful.

Among the most popular songs of this era was Elton John's "Philadelphia Freedom." Some of the other big hits that had Americans singing along were: Glen Campbell's "Rhinestone Cowboy," Morris Albert's "Feelings," and the Captain and Tennile's "Love Will Keep Us Together."

Steven Spielberg had us on the edge of our seats with his movie *Jaws*, Sylvester Stallone delivered his knockout *Rocky*, and Jack Nicholson made us wonder whether the inmates were really running the asylum in *One Flew Over the Cuckoo's Nest*.

On the track at Indianapolis, Johnny Rutherford was the man in 1974 and 1976, with Bobby Unser stepping up in the 1975 race. Other dominating performances during 1975-76 were put in by the Cincinnati Reds, who won back-to-back World Series championships, and the Pittsburgh Steelers, who repeated as Super Bowl victors.

The "America's Most Beautiful Roadsteræ title at the 1975 Oakland Roadster Show went to Lonnie Gilbertson, who rebuilt his '23 Ford roadster. In this

Mike Spangler's '28 Ford phaeton is looking good in the late afternoon sun. The lovely model was Mike's friend Connie White.

A tobacco-brown lacquer with black fenders is a pretty combination for this four-door touring car. Body and paint work is credited to Bob Davidson. The interior is dark-brown rolled and pleated Naugahyde.

This Ford was powered by a stock '74 Ford 2800-cc Capri V-6. The engine easily fit under the Model A hood. The V-6 is backed by a C-4 automatic transmission and a '63 Chevy Corvette rear end. The rear end was narrowed 4 inches to keep the Buick wire wheels and Firestone tires under the fenders.

Up front, a Maas 4-inch, tube-type dropped axle was used with split hairpin-style wishbones. The brakes are from a '63 Corvette and the shocks are tube type.

69

Can you identify this wild custom? It began as a 1965 Chevy Impala. Harry Bradley came up with the design for the owner, Bob Huffman. Prominent features are the extended nose and front fenders, and the use of 1/8x1/2-inch flat bar to create the grille. He mounted headlights behind the grille.

Bob Schoonhover of Vancouver, Washington, owned the car when I photographed it at the 1975 Los Angeles Winternationals Car Show. Schoonhover and Phil Schaffer chopped the top 2 1/2 inches, built the T-top roof with fiberglass inserts, installed suicide doors, and applied the candy burnt-orange lacquer. Hydraulics were used to lower the car. It rides on B.F. Goodrich tires and Zenith wire wheels. Jerry Rosell did the gold crushed-velvet interior.

reincarnation, the roadster came back with a yellow pearl, mural paint job, a hand-made front suspension, and a supercharged engine.

The "Sam Barris" award at the 1976 Sacramento Autorama was collected by Richard Zocchi for his chopped '50 Mercury coupe, known as the *Cool 50*.

Bob Sbarbaro won the 1976 Oakland Show title with his '23 Ford touring. He packed a supercharged 427 Cobra engine into one of Henry Ford's diminutive tourings, then painted it deep candy red and added Formula One wheels.

Is this beautiful '39 Chevy a custom or a low rider? A case could be made for either. I like the full-length chrome Lakes.

The paint and bodywork were done by the owner, Albert Provost, who chose a Metalflake gold body with Metalflake bronze fenders, roof, and highlights around the windows. Provost also completed the interior himself, in brown Naugahyde, with a brown frieze. The running boards were covered with brown carpet.

This cool two-door sedan was called *The Witness*.

Bruce McCoy's '33 Ford was awarded the National Street Rod Association's "Best Street Rod" trophy at the 1975 Los Angeles Winternationals Car Show.

The Tudor sedan has a '65 Corvair front suspension, Teco quick-steering arms, and a '72 Pinto rack-and-pinion steering. The 331-ci '69 Chevy engine gets some extra hop from a Sig Erson cam kit, Hank crankshaft, and an Edelbrock manifold with 650 Holley carburetor. A Rossi Superglide transmission is mated to a '70 Corvette rear end.

Inside is silver-gray, crushed-velvet, nylon cut-pile carpets. Stewart Warner gauges and an AM/FM stereo 8-track tape unit are in the dash.

Color and Design of El Monte can take a bow for painting—candy-red with pearl-gold base on the body, silver Alfa Metalflake on the fenders, and candy-red flames.

McCoy lives in Chino, California, and is a member of the Uniques Car Club of Pomona Valley.

**O**nly 979 four-door convertibles rolled off the Mercury assembly line in 1940. In 1975, this one made it to the Oakland Roadster Show.

Construction on this custom began in 1943 at Bertolucci's Body Shop in Sacramento, California. The owner was Harold "Buddy" Ohanesian, and at least some of the work was done by Harry Westergard. The job wasn't completed until 1946.

Bertolucci's shop chopped the windshield 4 inches, and fitted a custom, removable hard top with original sedan side-posts. The hood was nosed and extended to meet the '46 Chevy grille. The original bumpers were swapped for those from a '42 Chevy, the headlights were frenched, and chrome trim was removed.

A 276-ci '42 Mercury flathead with an Iskenderian cam, Edelbrock high-compression heads, Harmon & Collins ignition, and Fenton headers sure must have sounded good. The transmission is the original three-speed column shift with a Weber clutch. The 1975 owners were Louie Martin and Dennis Nash of Sacramento.

**T**his view of the '40 Mercury four-door convertible shows off the extensive work that was put into the removable hardtop. Notice the even spacing between the top and body. The rear window is from an early Plymouth.

The trunk opening was cut smaller to accommodate the new top, and the license plate was recessed and frenched into the trunk with glass covering the opening. The '42 Ford splash pan was extended and molded to the body, and the '42 Ford taillights received the same molded-in treatment. Early customizing tricks included extending the exhaust tips through the bumper, near the bumper guards. Also, '40 Packard teardrop fender skirts, popular at the time, were used here.

New Maroon lacquer paint was done by Dennis Nash. Maroon-and-white, pleated Naugahyde upholstery was restored by Ron Lago.

The steering wheel and dash are from a '41 Cadillac.

The sign reads:
DARRYL STARBIRD PRESENTS
STAR CAR CARAVAN
DARRYL STARBIRD'S
**VANTASTA**
500 HP CHEVIE V8 350 CU.IN.
ALL METAL HAND-FORMED BODY
FUTURISTICALLY DESIGNED &
STYLED, BUILT & PAINTED BY
JIM TROYER, DESIGNED BY
DARRYL STARBIRD, INTERIOR
WORK BY REX ADAMS.

**M**any of the cars in this book had chrome plating done by Joe the Chromer. Well, here he is. That's Joe Ross—with the cigar and the can of wax—attending to details prior to the opening of the Monterey Kar Kapades in February 1975.

And that's Joe's car, the '23 T with the 427-ci Ford engine, NASCAR-type intake, and tube-type headers with built-in mufflers. Everything on the underside of the car was chrome-plated.

The fiberglass body was the work of Steve Archer, and the pearl-yellow paint was done by Rod Powell. Bill Manger of Castroville gets credit for the brown top and upholstery. Firestone rain tires are mounted on Zenith wire wheels.

**C**ustom car builder Darryl Starbird of Mulvane, Kansas, came up with this promotional idea, a '74 Ford van he called *Vantasta*.

To get the desired shape, Starbird tore the body apart and began forming a framework. The all-metal, hand-formed body was constructed with 20-gauge, hammer-welded sheet metal and polished aluminum stock.

A pearl-white underbase with candy-purple paint was shot on by Jim Troyer based on artwork by Rex Adams of Crazy Paint in Kansas City, Missouri.

The front portion of *Vantasta*—where the driver and passenger sit—is a lift top. The seats are hand-built from aluminum and covered with white diamond-pleated Naugahyde upholstery. The carpets are blue.

The engine is a mid-mounted 350-ci Chevy with 500 horsepower. It's covered with a Lucite see-through box. *Vantasta* rides on Supersport M 50 14-inch tires on polished aluminum wheels.

Half Moon Bay has historical significance for many West Coast car buffs and hot rod enthusiasts because of the drag races once held there. Ten miles south of Half Moon Bay is San Gregorio State Beach, a favorite meeting ground for the Bay Area Roadster Club and the San Jose Roadsters.

This is Andy Brizio's chrome yellow '32 Ford roadster at the 1975 picnic. A 350-ci '73 Chevy engine is neatly tucked inside. The small block was balanced by Douglas Engineering, and it made good use of an Andy's combination blower. The exhaust headers were home made. A Turbo 400 transmission handled the horses. Disc brakes all around made stopping from cruising speed a lot easier.

Inside the upholstery is brown Naugahyde by Ken Foster of Sacramento. Nine Stewart Warner gauges are found in the dash.

On the road are Goodyear Polyglas GT tires mounted on Zenith wire wheels. If you are a louver counter, I'll save you some time. This one has 140 on the hood and side panels. C & M Plating of San Francisco did all the chrome.

My friend Greg Sharp of Hollywood, California, owned this wildly flamed '73 GMC Sierra Fleetside pickup.

Customizer Gene Winfield chopped the top 5 inches. The chop required removing a strip of metal down the middle of the roof and slanting the rear posts forward. This allowed the windshield to stay at its original angle. Of course, the doors were reworked to fit the new openings. Other modifications included some de-chroming, seam filling, and installing Ford remote-controlled side mirrors. Winfield shot the multicolored pearlescent flames, while famous pinstriper Kelly outlined edges in blue.

Pete & Jake's Hot Rod Repair lowered the truck more than one foot. As was the customizing trend of that era, the grille was blacked out. Modern Auto Trim of Whittier created the black, pleated Naugahyde upholstery and the tonneau cover for the bed. In case he needed to haul anything, a 454-ci Chevy with Edelbrock manifold and Holley carb could be called into action. American 200S mags were wrapped with Goodrich radials. Here Greg's pickup is shown at the 11th Annual L.A. Roadster Exhibition of 1975.

Usually I'm behind the camera taking pictures, but this time I'm getting photographed.

The blue-and-gold trim shirt was the latest model for my club, the Bay Area Roadsters. Beside me is my '32 Ford highboy roadster powered by a 283-ci Chevy with an automatic transmission, '56 Ford station wagon rear end with 3.56 ratio, and coil spring rear suspension.

Walking through the swap meet area of the 1975 L.A. Roadsters Car Show, I was impressed when I saw this chopped and channeled black beauty.

From the windshield forward, this was '40 Ford; rearward from the windshield was a '39 Ford convertible with a rumble seat. It was unusual to see this combination, but it looked great!

The windshield was chopped 3 inches, the body was channeled over the frame, and the hood was sectioned. The interior had black Naugahyde upholstery, and a dash that was semicustom '40 Ford. A padded Carson top gives the car a unique look.

Tom Rock of Los Alamitos, California, was the owner. He chose a 289 Ford engine with a C-4 transmission for his drivetrain.

photographed this gorgeous '34 Ford sedan delivery in the swap meet area of the L.A. Roadster Exhibition in June 1975.

The car belonged to Don Thelen of Bellflower, California. Ron Jones did some body work and painted the dark-green lacquer with apple trim. The delivery area of this sedan delivery has superb oak flooring that is hand-finished and highly polished.

Tan Naugahyde with brown suede-like inserts and matching carpeting was the choice for interior materials. A burled dashboard was restored with new old-stock gauges.

The front end is lowered by a Bell dropped axle. The spindles and brakes come from a '40 Ford. A custom steering wheel operates the Mustang steering box. Pete & Jake did the chassis work, and installed the 302-ci Ford engine with automatic transmission. The rear end was taken from a '57 Ford with semielliptic springs. The wire wheels with traditional skinny tires are early Ford.

If you put it to a vote, an old-fashioned '32 Ford highboy roadster would be the number one choice of most hot rodders. This one, owned by Bob Dyar of Phoenix, Arizona, is an uncommon example of a familiar roadster. It is unusual in that it is painted all white, a nice job by Dyar's friend, Dick Smith.

Another unique item is the one-piece removable hard top, covered with red Naugahyde. The interior, done by Bill Swenson, features red, pleated Naugahyde seats and door panels, red carpets, and a red dashboard that is home to a speedometer and six Stewart Warner gauges.

One other item rarely seen on a highboy is air conditioning.

Power to drive the air-conditioning compressor comes from a 284-ci '48 Ford engine. An Offenhauser intake manifold with two chrome-plated Stromberg 97 carbs sits atop the flathead. An aluminum Schiefer flywheel, with clutch disc and pressure plate, gives power to a '39 Ford transmission with Zephyr gears. All four brakes are from a '40 Ford.

Bob Haddad of Tarzana, California, owned this 4-inch chop-top '34 Ford coupe. Although Haddad was a parts manager for a Ford dealership, his choice of engines was a 283-ci Chevy, with a C & T crankshaft, Chevy 097 cam, and a full Cragar blower drive with a 471 GMC blower. The transmission was a B & M Hydra-matic matched up with a '65 Mustang rear end with 4.11 gears. The brakes and suspension are from a '40 Ford, and the steering unit came from a '55 Ford pickup.

Jack's Top Shop of Tarzana upholstered the car in pleated black Naugahyde. The Cortina GT instruments are not something you would see very often. Paint colors are burnt cinnamon and midnight bronze. The combination of Firestone Wide Ovals and Ansen aluminum wheels look great!

Bob was president of the Hard Times Car Club of Southern California.

This custom-in-progress, a '40 Chevy convertible owned by Ron Brooks of San Lorenzo, California, shows a variety of custom features.

1) The stock grille cavity was reworked to fit a modified '49 Cadillac grille and straight bar. 2) The hood was shaved of chrome and filled. 3) The door handles were removed and the doors were rigged to open with electric solenoids. 4) The running boards were removed and a cover between frame and fenders was fabricated. 5) A chrome shield was fitted to the front of the rear fender. 6) The windshield was chopped and a custom convertible top was made by King Kovers of Hayward, California. 7) The upholstery was done in black, button-tufted Naugahyde, and the trunk had cut-pile rugs to match the interior. 8) A custom lacquer paint was mixed in the color of deep mahogany. 9) A GMC six-cylinder engine was set up with an Edelbrock manifold and dual one-barrel carbs.

A total of 790 street rods and customs participated in the 1975 West Coast Championship Rod Run at Lodi, California, where this picture was taken.

When you went to a roadster roundup back in the '70s, all you saw were roadsters! I participated in a roadster roundup in Santa Maria, California, on September 13, 1975, with my '32 Ford roadster.

San Jose Roadster Club member Sil Moyano of Campbell, California, was there with his maroon '35 Ford phaeton. The phaeton body style is a four-door convertible without roll-up windows, but Sil had a complete set of side curtains in case the weather turned foul. The handsome, custom-padded Carson top on this car was done by Hall's of Oakland, California. The top can be removed as one piece. Hall's was also credited with the fine rolled and pleated black Naugahyde upholstery.

The hood was punched with 60 louvers; the door handles were taken off; and the windshield was chopped 3 inches.

The front axle is a 3-inch dropped '41 Ford. A 327-ci Chevy gets things going. It's mated with a '39 Ford transmission and a '41 Ford rear end.

Here's a seldom-seen custom—a '39 Ford four-door convertible sedan. It was owned by John Karr, a member of a car club known as the Over the Hill Gang.

This custom was lowered so much the front fender wells had to be enlarged so the tires would clear on tight turns. The combination of chromed reversed wheels and baldy hubcaps looks great. Notice the skinny whitewalls of the 1970s era. Smooth gray carpeting covered the running boards.

All side trim was discarded, and the door handles were removed. The quad headlights were frenched and semitunneled into the fenders. The sheet metal was extended from the lower portion of the hood, conforming to the shape of the '46 Chevy grille. A light-tan Naugahyde upholstery and a white top were good complementary choices. The '41 Studebaker taillights were vertically mounted to conform with the shape of the fenders.

A '56 Oldsmobile engine was under the hood.

Originally built in Texas, this '34 Ford roadster has really gotten around.

Bay Area Roadster member Ed Lee, who currently owns the car, related some of the history. When it was originally customized, the windshield was chopped 2 1/2 inches. It was fitted with a black top, and Beef Eater wide-pleated, black Naugahyde upholstery.

The engine was a 301-ci Chevy with a Holley four-barrel carb on a Weiand manifold. A four-speed transmission was hooked into a '57 Chevy rear end. The chromed wire wheels are from a Buick.

From Texas, the car went to Los Angeles, then to San Luis Obispo, where Keith and Bud Bryson were owners. Keith was at the Roadster Roundup on September 13, 1975, in Santa Maria, California, where this picture was taken.

Well, looka here! Jerry Stich and Andy Brizio (driving) are cruisin' in Brizio's '23 T roadster at the 1975 roadster roundup in Santa Maria.

Because Andy was so busy with his business, he had John Buttera put this chassis together, along with other components, to almost complete the roadster. The body is fiberglass. Steve Davis of Paramount, California, did all the aluminum bending: full belly pan, gas tank, and hood. Jack Hagemann punched the louvers on the hood and side panels.

Steve Archer did additional body work, and painted the roadster white with a new process called electrostatic powder coating. Tommy the Greek did minor scallops and the pinstriping, and Ken Foster did the orange Naugahyde upholstery. Up front is a Bell tube dropped axle, custom disc brakes, and Vega steering. TRW shocks are used in front, with Porsche Carrera coil-overs in rear.

And how's this for an engine surprise? It's a '74 Mazda Rotary, joined with a Mazda transmission and a narrowed '57 Chevy rear end.

One of the Bay Area Roadster Club's regular cruises was the Seventeen Mile Drive in Pebble Beach, California.

While there was a break in the action, I photographed this 1915 steel body Ford roadster pickup owned by Ray Lenz of San Leandro. Fellow club member Tony Martinez assisted Lenz in building this project. Some of their modifications include a rectangular tube frame, using a dropped '32 front axle with leaf springs and tubular radius rods. The front spindles and brakes are from a '48 Ford, steering is a Morris Minor rack-and-pinion unit, and the rear end is from a '66 Chevy with coil springs. Lenz runs on Goodyear Sports tires mounted on polished American mag wheels.

A stock 302-ci Chevy provides the power. It is fitted with F-1 heads, and an Edelbrock manifold with a four-barrel carb. Homemade headers route Cherry Bomb mufflers underneath the roadster. The transmission is a Turbo-Hydra-matic. In typical customizer fashion, black tufted Naugahyde is the chosen upholstery and Stewart Warner gauges were used in the dash. The original 1917 T cowl lamps are chromed and wired for directional signals.

Although you might be fooled into thinking this is a '34 Ford, it's not. The hood and the grille shell are from a '34, but the rest of the body is vintage 1933. This Tudor sedan belongs to Red Spence, who was wiping off the dust when I photographed it on August 23, 1975. A beautiful crimson-red lacquer and a light-gold pinstriping are a great combo on this car.

Jerry Kugel of Los Angeles built the rigid box frame. Chassis components have a lot of Jaguar in them, including the front and rear suspension, the rack-and-pinion steering, and the brakes.

The engine is a stock 283-ci Chevy with a Powerglide transmission.

Buick Skylark chrome wire wheels dress up the big and little tires. A combination of brown Naugahyde and Herculon tweed fabrics are used in the interior.

**H**ere, at the 1974 San Jose Autorama, is the rear of Don Varner's '29 Ford road-ster pickup, with the mirror on the floor giving a view of the XKE Jaguar 3.78 rear end. Notice that the tailgate has a tube grille, which follows the same design theme as the front grille shell. The pickup bed was sectioned 10 inches, which brought the tailgate closer to the rear fenders. The rear portions of the fenders have been shortened 4 inches. Dual '29-style taillights have custom, upward-curved brackets. Square exhaust tips extend past the bed, and between the split bumpers. The running boards have aluminum step plates.

Ken Foster of A Action upholstery in Sacramento worked out the rolled and pleated Naugahyde, and the custom one-piece, lift-off top. Dash is an Auburn type with five gauges. Notice the polished mag wheels prior to the wire wheels of 1975.

**W**hat would Henry Ford have thought about the lavish attention given to one of his more humble vehicles, a '29 Ford roadster pickup? I think he would have been pleased with the enthusiasm and the ingenuity displayed.

For instance, this roadster pickup has a tube space frame custom-built by Greg Turretto, a fully chrome-plated Jaguar XKE suspension, plus adjustable torsion bars and Monroe shocks. The engine is a 289-ci Ford Cobra with two four-barrel carbs. That's bolted to a T-10 Ford four-speed transmission with a Weber clutch and flywheel. Gas is carried in two Ron Covell 10-gallon aluminum side tanks. The underside has an aluminum belly pan.

Body modifications include a Jack Hagemann-built three-piece hood with louvers in the side panels, and a '32 Ford grille shell with a custom-made tube-type grille. Notice how the headlight bar extends through the grille shell. The Model A front apron is chromed, and the bumper is a custom job.

Owner Don Varner of Morgan Hill, California, is a talented painter, as you can see with the job he did on his '29 Ford, using BMC black tulip lacquer. He also did the pinstriping.

That's Don in the blue shirt, and Bob Barnes, an L.A. Roadster member, to the right.

If memory serves me right, this was the third roadster I striped for Tom Prufer. His cars are always first class, and I am honored to be asked to stripe for him.

This '29 Ford roadster is painted black-cherry pearl lacquer, and I'm striping in gold. In addition to striping the '32 Ford grille shell, shown here, I did the body moldings and some simple patterns around the taillights. And, oh yeah, I had fun doing the tops of the 140 louvers on the hood and side panels. The trunk lid even had 5 rows of louvers, with a total count of 80.

Three weeks after I pinstriped Prufer's '29 Ford roadster, I was back, shooting pictures for a feature article that was published in the September 1976 issue of *Rod Action* magazine.

Prufer's roadster was set up on a '32 Ford frame. Pete & Jakes Hot Rod Repair of Temple City, California, handled those duties. A '32 Ford dropped axle, Model A Ford springs, and chrome tube shocks were also part of the project. The steering assembly came from a Chevy Vega.

The engine is a '73 Ford 351, matched up with a C-4 automatic transmission and a C.A.E. Championship quick-change rear end, with a trick A-spring mount above the axle housings. Brakes, front and rear, are C.A.E./Airheart discs. Big and little Firestone tires on polished Halibrand wheels give the car that classic look.

Additional nice touches include a Jack Hagemann-fabricated three-piece hood with louvers, a chopped windshield, and GTO taillights mounted below the trunk. The beautiful black-cherry pearl paint was laid on by Johnson Brothers of San Jose. Inside, the '32 Ford dash is modified with Stewart Warner gauges, the upholstery is dark-brown Naugahyde, and if you're lucky enough to be the one driving, you grab a Grant steering wheel.

You could call Rod Powell the human flame-thrower. This guy can flat-out paint up a firestorm. This customized '56 Chevy sedan delivery just happens to be his own car.

Rod bought the Chevy from Rocky DeMateo because he liked the 3-inch chop top, and he wanted a "shop truck." Obviously his vision of a shop truck, to represent Rod Powell's Custom Painting, is somewhat different than the average Joe's. Nothing run-of-the-mill would do.

The body needed only minor work—a little straightening made things right, and the hood ornament needed to disappear. Jack Bradford, who worked for Rod, sprayed the black lacquer. Rod, of course, did the flames, using yellow and orange pearl, and the edges were pinstriped in light blue.

Allen Signs took care of the lettering and rechroming was done by Salinas Plating Co. The upholstery was done in pleated, flat-black Naugahyde.

A 283-ci Chevy engine and transmission make the chromed reversed wheels with Shannon cone hubcaps go round.

**A** collaboration of two great custom car designers, Harry Bradley and Herb Gary, produced this outstanding '51 Chevy Bel Air hardtop, named *La Jolla*.

The rear half of this car is channeled, the frame is stepped, and the flooring in the rear seat and trunk area is raised. Lowering was accomplished by cutting the front springs, and using reversed rear-spring eyes. The top was chopped 3 1/2 inches in front and 3 3/4 inches in the rear.

Other features include a '53 Pontiac one-piece windshield, and a narrowed and chopped '49 Plymouth rear window. The hood was molded to the body, and new openings were cut. Frenched headlights, a '49 Merc grille shell with copper grille insert, and custom Lucite taillights combine to make this car a custom showcase.

Deep chocolate mahogany pearl lacquer was chosen for the paint, and the interior is champagne-colored Naugahyde with matching velvet inserts.

The engine, Powerglide, and rear end are from a '57 Chevy.

I first met Dick Eaton in 1972, when he wanted me to pinstripe his '32 Ford sedan. Since then we have been friends.

Dick was in the military, and he moved around the country. In 1973, he got the word he was going to Nebraska. Although he didn't know when he would be back in California, he had Jack Hagemann do a three-piece hood for his newly acquired roadster. In late 1974, he moved to Alabama and finished the roadster there.

I took this picture on March 14, 1976. Dick is smiling because he's back in California roadster country. His '32 was painted candy Nile green. Butch Winsett of Huntsville, Alabama, gets the credit. Auto Center in Huntsville upholstered the car in brown Naugahyde.

The engine is a stock 289 from a '67 Ford. It's backed by a C-4 automatic transmission and a complete '68 Jaguar rear end. The front end is a bolt-in '68 Jaguar, with Morris Minor rack-and-pinion steering.

One of the nicest roadsters I've ever photographed is Gil Ferreira's '29 Ford. Gil did a major portion of the work, but other famous people had a hand in it, such as Greg Turretto, who made the space-age frame by hand from 1 1/2-inch square tubing.

The front end has a Bell dropped tube axle with '62 Corvette spindles and Porsche disc brakes. The front radius rods are the split hairpin style. The shocks are MG fluid-type, and the steering box is a '74 Saginaw unit.

Ron Covell did the custom horizontal grille bars, chromed splash apron, aluminum hood, and side panels, with 66 louvers on each panel. Other classic features include the thin nerf-type bumpers, the headlight bar intersecting the '32 Ford grille shell, and the custom-made running boards. Henry Hurlhey of Rod Powell's shop did the body work.

Sky Clausen shot the '76 Lincoln dark-brown metallic paint, Paul Vona did the orange pinstriping, and Ken Foster was the upholstery guy who laid on the pleated buckskin Naugahyde.

Jerry Stich calls his '29 Model A Ford a good old-fashioned street roadster of the 1970s.

The front end has a 3 1/2-inch dropped axle, with split hairpin-style wishbones, plus disc brakes and steering gear from a '65 Mustang. The three-piece hood was made by Jack Hagemann. There are 36 louvers on top and 86 louvers on the side panels. The original gas tank filler on the cowl was filled, as was the '32 Ford grille shell. He prefers the look of the dropped headlight bar and the big and little 15-inch tires.

Under the hood is a 327-ci '73 Chevy, with four-barrel carburetor. It's mated to a Powerglide automatic transmission. Ken Foster did the tan Naugahyde upholstery.

Gil Ferreira is checking out the carburetor linkage on his 283-ci Chevy. The small block has a Carter AFB carburetor on an Edelbrock manifold, Mallory ignition, and porcelainized exhaust headers. The valve covers are finned, polished aluminum.

The transmission is a Turbo 350 automatic, backed up to a completely chromed Jaguar rear end. Radial tires are mounted on Zenith wire wheels. Oh, yes, '41 Chevy taillights are molded into bobbed rear fenders. A small, rolled rear pan is underneath the body. The stylish dash is from a '32 Auburn. It has a polished center panel with a speedometer and four Stewart Warner gauges.

Jerry Stich's roadster top and spare tire cover were made by Ken Foster. The rear bumpers are stock.

A '65 Mustang rear end was narrowed 4 inches and mounted with Jaguar coil-over-shocks and four-bar radius rods. The interior is highlighted by a deep-set classic Auburn dash with five gauges. The steering column is from a Mustang, and a Hurst shifter is on the floor.

I suppose you thought I'd never get around to telling you who this pretty model is. Her name is Cathy Navarro, and you may have seen her in TV commercials for Coca-Cola and AMC. She has also been in print ads for Black Velvet liquor, Ditto Jeans, and *Vogue* magazine.

# Chapter

# 4

# 1977-1979

Of all the events that occurred in the late 1970s, the one that perhaps rocked the most people was the death of rock 'n' roll legend Elvis Presley on August 16, 1977. He was a uniquely American icon who was recognized throughout the world. And to his millions of fans, he will always be "The King."

Yet another incredibly magnetic personality, and someone who gained an even greater amount of worldwide acclaim, was the irrepressible Muhammad Ali. In 1978, Ali won the heavyweight championship of the world for an unprecedented third time.

The final years of the up-and-down 1970s also brought the first execution in the United States in 10 years, when convicted murderer Gary Gilmore was killed by a firing squad in Utah. The surgeon general warned us of the harmful effects of smoking tobacco, and Three Mile Island nuclear energy plant gave us a scare of its own.

A second energy crisis of the decade put another burr under our saddle and dent in our pocketbook. And, not coincidentally, General Motors was preparing to introduce diesel-engined Oldsmobiles with a claimed 40 percent increase in fuel mileage. The biggest news from the auto industry was the government-approved $1.5 billion bailout of Chrysler.

At the box office, movie-goers were treated to *Star Wars*, *Close Encounters of the Third Kind*, *The Deer Hunter*, and *Grease*.

Bill Burnham of Danville, California, was a major contributor to the San Francisco Bay Area hot rod and custom scene. In 1994 he was inducted into the Oakland Roadster Show Hall of Fame. His involvement with that tradition-rich event contributed greatly to its blossoming success. Burnham's first "good" car in the show was a '32 Ford sedan entered in 1954.

I had the privilege of knowing Bill Burnham, and on July 4, 1977, I photographed his frost-turquoise 1929 Ford roadster that he called *Old Blue*. I knew Bill a long time, and my good friend passed away on August 24, 1996.

Bill's "hot rod" (he always referred to his cars as hot rods), had a Ford 406-ci engine with dual Carter AFB carbs. The transmission was stock C-6 Ford unit mated to a '64 Thunderbird rear end. The front axle was dropped and chromed. It featured a Jack Hagemann three-piece hood, and pinstripes by Tommy the Greek. *Old Blue*'s upholstery was tan Naugahyde and suede. The wheels are from a '49 Ford, and the front brakes are '48 Ford.

How low can you go?

When I first saw this 1966 Chevy Caprice coupe, I couldn't believe the height. From top to bottom, it's only 3-feet, 9-inches high. The owner, Nash Ramos of Fresno, California, came up with a name that turned out to be prophetic. He called it *California Lowrider*.

Ramos and the Mercado Brothers, also of Fresno, began by chopping 4 1/2-inches from the top. They also laid back the windshield posts to a 60-degree angle and moved them inward 1 1/2 inches to accommodate a '67 Cadillac windshield. The rear window was set 2 inches into the top, which required 20 cuts to give the roofline a pleasing slope. This modification necessitated shortening the body panel under the rear window and rear package tray. Side wind wings were eliminated.

A slight flaring of the fender wells provides clearance for 14-inch radials on Tru-Spoke wire wheels. Black lacquer paint with candy-red flames was nicely done by Ron Schramek of Clovis.

Debbie Boone, daughter of 1950s crooner Pat Boone, had a Number One hit in 1977 with "You Light Up My Life." The Bee Gees continued their resurgence with "How Deep Is Your Love," and Andy Gibb, a Bee Gee gone solo, serenaded us with "I Just Want to be Your Everything."

The 1977 Indianapolis 500 crowd witnessed history as A. J. Foyt won his fourth crown and female driver Janet Guthrie was in the starting grid. Al Unser picked up his third Indy victory in 1978, and Rick Mears got his first in 1979.

When the New York Yankees won the 1977 World Series, it was the first since 1962 for that storied franchise. A repeat in 1978 made things even sweeter in the Big Apple. Pittsburgh was on top of the sporting world in 1979 when the Pirates won the World Series and the Steelers won their third Super Bowl of the 1970s.

In the hot rod world, Jim Moleno's *Candy Man*, a tall-top T roadster, won top honors at the 1977 Oakland Roadster Show. The trend at this time was candy-colored paints and plenty of glittering chrome. In a break with the popular trends, Phil Cool, in 1978, took the "AMBR" award with his '32 Ford highboy roadster. It was only the second time a '32 had won the title since 1956.

Ken Nannenhorn of Brookfield, Wisconsin, won the "Sam Barris" award at the 1979 Sacramento Autorama. His '26 Ford was called the *King's Coupe*. The 1979 winner at the Oakland Roadster Show was Brian Burnett's '32 Ford roadster. Burnett threw tradition out the window by powering his roadster with a Ferrari V-12 engine.

# 1970s

## OAKLAND ROADSTER SHOW WINNERS

1970 Andy Brizio, *Instant T*, 1923 Ford fiberglass roadster

1971 Lonnie Gilbertson, 1923 T Ford fiberglass roadster

1972 John Corno, 1930 Ford roadster

1973 Chuck Corsello, 1923 T Ford fiberglass roadster

1974 Jim Vasser, 1923 T Ford fiberglass touring

1975 Lonnie Gilbertson, 1923 T Ford fiberglass roadster

1976 Bob Sbarbaro, 1923 T Ford fiberglass touring

1977 Jim Molino, *Candy Man* 1923 T Ford fiberglass roadster

1978 Phil Cool, 1932 Ford roadster

1979 Brian Burnett, 1932 Ford roadster

Lowering the coupe meant more than just being chopped. It took four guys to get the body off the frame so it could be channeled. After channeling, it was 2 inches lower than original. The trunk area lost 8 inches of depth. As low as it got, it maintained a decent ride and handling.

Lupe's of Highway City, California, created the black Naugahyde interior. It had hundreds of buttons and diamond pleats that covered the bucket seats, door panels, and headliner. Black imitation fur covered the trunk area. For comfortable driving, the steering column and seats were lowered.

De-chroming of all stock trim, door handles, and filling in all the factory seams, gave the body that one-piece look. Even the bumper bolts were filled.

Ramos' next-door neighbor, 18-year-old Rhonda Hall, was a custom car enthusiast, and wanted to pose pretty for pictures on February 12, 1977.

A little over two decades ago, I met Loren "Curley" Tremayne of New Monterey, California.

Tremayne was working at Rod Powell's shop when I first met him, and his dream car was a chopped '50 Merc. Well, this is proof that dreams can come true. Curley got his car, and with the help of Henry "Butch" Hurlhey, they chopped 3 1/2 inches from the front and 5 1/2 inches from the rear. Numerous cuts and fittings were made to get the elusive perfect roof slant. The door posts were slanted forward, enhancing the sleek appearance.

All the trim pieces, emblems, and door handles were removed. The hood and deck lid corners were rounded. A wire mesh grille with a "floating" '63 Buick Wildcat bar is used to good effect. The headlights were frenched, using '53 Buick headlight rims. The power was generated by a '55 Y-block Ford.

That's Curley in the car talking with Laura Buss of Santa Cruz. Sadly, Curley passed away May 31, 1998.

A three-quarter rear view of Curley's chopped '50 Mercury coupe shows the nice slope of the roof line. Due to the chop, additional metal is placed between the trunk and the rear window.

Because the trunk lid is de-chromed, Paul "Stroker" Lewis converted it to open hydraulically with '68 Chevy convertible lifts. Paul was also responsible for the solenoid-operated doors. Taillights are frenched, using '53 Buick units. The cool trend at the time was using full-length chrome Lakes pipes. Curley's choice of hubcaps came from a '54 Oldsmobile. The wide whitewall tires are Bedfords.

The master of the paint gun, Rod Powell, laid on the outstanding candy-tangerine lacquer paint, highlighted with candy-apple red. White Naugahyde pearl upholstery was fashioned by Rocky and Ron's upholstery. I wish you could have seen the white shag carpets.

Don Varner gets paid to come up with good ideas—he's an industrial designer by profession. He's also a hot rodder in his heart, so it should come as no surprise that Varner came up with an idea for a fabulous '23 T roadster.

John Buttera of Los Angeles built the chrome moly frame of rectangular tubing. Ron Covell and Sam Davis fabricated the aluminum and many detailed parts. Covell also chopped 5 inches from the roadster's windshield posts. Steve Archer took Varner's ideas and turned them into a fiberglass body.

Varner painted the roadster jet-black lacquer, and when it was time to get it "flamed" he called on Rod Powell.

I took this picture of Rod painting the multiple colors that went into the flames.

An article about Don Varner in the December 1956 issue of *Rod & Custom* referred to him as "The Northwest Striping King."

When I first met Don he was pinstriping a '39 Chevy coupe owned by Rod Powell. That is also where I first met Rod Powell, and we have been close friends ever since.

It's ironic that years later (see previous picture) Rod would be taping, flaming, and painting for Don Varner. Not many pictures have been taken of Don pinstriping. I'm pleased that I can show you my March 20, 1977, picture of Don in action. With all those louvers and flames, many hours were spent striping in gold.

When the Johnson Brothers had a custom body shop in Campbell, California, one of the brothers, Bob, had a '59 Ford Ranchero pickup, and decided to customize it to show people what he could do.

He chopped the top 3 1/2 inches, retaining the original lines without having to slant the windshield posts. A 1 1/2-inch piece of metal was put into place in the center of the roof to make up the difference. The stock window glass was cut down to fit.

The front fenders were sectioned and hand-formed so that a '57 Thunderbird hood, with a modified air scoop, would match. Frenched '53 Ford headlight rims, with '62 Chrysler parking lights, framed the hand-formed grille cavity. The chrome frame for the grille was made from the rear deck-lid grille of a Porsche 911. Under the hood is a '68 Cobra engine. The remainder of the driveline was a Ford four-speed transmission and the original Ranchero rear end.

The Ranchero frame was shortened 12 inches, which also reduced the wheelbase to 112 inches. Two feet were carved off the original Ranchero truck bed, and rear quarter panels were fabricated from sheet metal and tubing, made to match a '67 Mustang rear body panel. The tailgate was molded into the truck bed, and a sunken license plate housing was incorporated into the tailgate. A stainless steel gas tank sits in the bed, with a racing-type filler cap protruding through the sturdy black Naugahyde padded tonneau cover.

Door handles were removed, and doors were opened electrically. The doors also were sectioned 2 1/2 inches to clear the functional '67 Corvette side exhausts, which were frenched into the body. Fender wells were flared to make room for Goodyear tires mounted on American Vector mag wheels.

Bob chose to paint the truck with black Imron paint, and then add flames in blue and silver. I was asked to pinstripe the pickup, including the flame edges.

103

Don Varner's concept of the ultimate '23 T roadster, unlike so many ideas that never make it beyond the doodling stage, made a stunning presentation. Several things grabbed my attention. The center hood louvers extended to the windshield by means of a louvered metal insert through the cowl. And custom outside chromed headers, made by Ron Covell, provided a smooth, blended look.

This roadster sits extremely low. Road clearance is 12 inches in the rear and 3 inches in the front. Attention to the details shows with the dropped tube front axle, Halibrand hubs, true knock-off wheels, PSI calipers, and Porsche rotors. Four-bar chromed wishbones were affixed to the frame.

A Mazda shifter actuates the C-4 Ford automatic transmission. The rear end is a Halibrand quick-change center section with 3.78 gears and blanked-out spur gears. The rear suspension has Carrera coil-over-shocks.

The black Naugahyde upholstery was done by Dave Putman of Sacramento.

On Saturday, May 1, 1977, when I photographed the completed roadster, it was a beautiful day to shoot pictures of a roadster, a fellow Bay Area Roadster member, and a model.

This 1977 photo is a posed shot with Don Varner kneeling and his daughter Kim posing by the engine compartment. I'm the guy with the 35-millimeter camera.

With a wrench in hand, Kim was showing how easy it was to tighten a bolt on the 2.3-liter V-6 Capri engine. Feeding the engine is a four-barrel carb on an Offenhauser manifold. Inside the V-6 is a DeLong camshaft with solid lifters.

The nosepiece of this roadster features a custom-chromed grille, three-piece hood, and multilouvered full belly pans constructed of aluminum by Ron Covell and Sam Davis. Firestone tires are mounted on highly polished Halibrand wheels.

Some car people take their cars very personally. Joe Garcia, who owns this '32 Ford roadster, once said to me, "Andy, I built this car myself. If I would have bought one completed, it would always be the other person's car and not mine." His sentiments are echoed by a lot of car people I know.

Garcia's '32 Ford has a steel body with only a few minor alterations. The door and trunk handles were removed, and the cowl air vent and grille shell were filled. The orange, yellow, blue, magenta, and purple flames with blue pinstriping were done by Mike Farley of San Mateo.

More alterations were made under the sheet metal. The front end has a dropped 3 1/2-inch chromed front axle. The steering unit is from a '57 Volkswagen bus, the brakes are from a '64 Econoline, and tube shocks are chromed TRW road huggers. Wheels and tires are '53 Chrysler painted wires with Dayton radials.

The engine is a stock 327-ci '65 Chevy with an Offenhauser manifold and Carter AFB carburetor.

While on the prowl for photographic subjects at the 1977 Lodi Nationals, I couldn't resist this superb maroon '40 Ford convertible, owned by Ron Glaser of Lafayette, California.

The top had been chopped about 2 1/2-inches, and the Carson-style convertible top added a lot of class.

The trunk was filled smooth, the hood was nosed, and the door handles removed. Classic teardrop style fender skirts make this a she's-so-fine-looking ride.

Cherry fizz lacquer is the color of this '48 Ford coupe. That comes straight from the source—owner/customizer Sam Foose of Goleta, California. Foose is serious about his paint. He said 20 hours were put into painting and rubbing out the unique "checker boards" on the firewall.

Sam's coupe is smooth. It had 3 inches chopped from the roof in front and 5 inches at the rear. The grille was filled and frenched, headlights were frenched with new housings, and parking lights were removed. In addition, front and rear gravel pans were molded into the body. The hood was nosed, and the door handles and side trim moldings were removed. Front and rear fenders were molded to the body.

Chrome sparkles everywhere on the 276-ci Ford flathead. On the business side, dual carbs, Jahns pistons, a 1/4-inch stroker crankshaft, and an Iskenderian full race cam combine to deliver 250 horsepower.

An outstanding interior in white leather and maroon Mohair was fashioned by John Englehart.

▌ didn't get the name of the lady sleeping in this '23 Ford touring, but I do know that the T belonged to Pete Orlando of Gilroy, California.

Nicknamed *Aquarius*, this touring sits on an Andy Brizio Instant T chassis. The custom accessories included a fully chromed front end and a dropped axle. The engine is a balanced and blueprinted 327-ci Chevy, topped with a Holley 650-cfm carburetor. Custom-chromed headers are by Sanderson. An Ansen shifter commanded a Powerglide transmission.

Black, button-and-tufted Naugahyde upholstery was the work of Ken Foster. Credit for the paint goes to Himsl & Haas.

**A** longtime friend, Bob Kraus, from North Babylon, New York, owned this channeled '32 Ford coupe. It had been upgraded nicely since the last time I had seen it, 12 years earlier in September 1965.

Bob is an excellent bodyman and was responsible for channeling the body the width of the frame. Additional custom bodywork includes a molded cowl air vent, and a recessed license plate in the rear panel. The taillights are Chevy. His super-straight coupe was painted a metallic forest-green lacquer. I did the honors of pinstriping the grille shell and rear deck.

A chromed, 2 1/2-inch dropped axle with split wishbones is up front. Tube shocks are chromed, as are the '32 headlight housings with sealed-beam lights inside.

The engine is a 322-ci Buick with an Offenhauser intake manifold and three 94 carburetors. A floor-mounted Chevy four-speed is linked to a '56 Chevy rear end with four-bar radius rods. The 15-inch tires and wheels are dressed up with baldy hubcaps.

A black diamond-pleated Naugahyde interior was created by Ed Geyer of Recovery Room Upholstery in Hicksville, New York. The stock dash has Stewart Warner gauges.

In the summer of 1977, I made a trip to New York and was introduced to Lou Muller of Amityville, on Long Island.

Muller's mint-green pearl 1937 Ford club coupe caught my attention, and now I think it will catch yours. The body is pretty much stock, except for the '63 Corvette taillights tucked into the rear fenders, 6 louvers on the lower portion of the front fenders, and 18 louvers on top of the hood.

Underneath that hood is a 302-ci Ford. It is hooked up to a C-4 transmission with a Mustang rear end. Chrome Lakes pipes protrude from under the fenderwell next to the padded running boards. A 2 1/2-inch, '37 Ford dropped axle and a set of PSI disc brakes are found up front.

The interior fabric is pearl-white Naugahyde done by L & B Upholstery. The dash is laminated walnut with Stewart Warner gauges.

This may have all the appearances of a 1950s custom job, but it is, in fact, a mid-1970s project. Alan Asnicar of Vallejo, California, bought a stock '51 Mercury in 1975 and jumped right in to a full-blown customizing undertaking. I took this picture in October 1977.

The chopped Merc in the classic film *American Graffiti* was an inspiration to Asnicar. He had seen chop jobs of three, four, and five inches, but he chose to get really radical and go for six inches. "Dirty Harry" of Vallejo Body Works did the radical chop top.

Other 1950s-era custom touches include a molded and louvered hood, fender skirts, frenched headlights, a '53 Chevy grille, and '55 Buick side trim. Jeff's Rods & Customs shop did the candy-red and silver paint. The interior has pearl-white Naugahyde upholstery.

**P**rimed, not painted, but looking as if it belongs in any 1950s street scene is this chop top '51 Mercury owned by Red Spence.

Red used a '40 DeSoto rear window, a grille from a '53 DeSoto, and bumperettes from a '51 Kaiser to protect the stock Merc bumper.

Door handles were removed and headlights and taillights ('56 Buick) were frenched. Butch Hurlhey of Salinas did the body work.

To get that low look, a C-frame was used in the rear with 3 1/2-inch blocks and flattened springs. Chromed wire wheels are vintage '53 Buick Skylark. Upholstery is purple Naugahyde.

This photo was shot at Rod Powell's 1977 picnic at Royal Oaks Park in Prunedale, California. Red Spence, his wife, Lee Anna, and daughter, Christy, can be seen looking through the small windows.

I have heard of roadsters being built in homes, but this was the first time I ever witnessed it. This is Phil Cool, polishing a Halibrand mag wheel, with pieces of his '32 Ford roadster spread around his very 1970s-looking home.

You can see he is working on a front wheel because the bigger back wheels are under the frame in the background. The frame is upside down, on stands, basking in the sunlight coming through his front window.

About a year had gone by since Phil Cool was photographed in his living room with his roadster in pieces. Here it is in February 1978. It had just won the "America's Most Beautiful Roadster" title at the Oakland Roadster Show.

It took Phil four years to build. Along the way he learned how to weld, fabricate and paint. Apparently he learned quite well.

His choice of paint was R & M moly orange acrylic lacquer. Nothing subtle about that. The black top and Naugahyde upholstery were done by Ken Foster.

The hood is louvered, the windshield is chopped, and there are '39 Ford taillights in the rear panel.

A Super Bell, 3-inch dropped axle with '49 Chevy spindles and Hurst/ Airheart double-puck disc brakes are on the front, and Hurst/Airheart single-puck discs are on the '57 Olds rear end. Split, chromed wishbones are used front and rear.

It's got the 3.70 Posi-Traction gears to go with a 427-ci '76 Chevy L-88 engine. Other goodies include an Iskenderian cam, a 10-percent-under-driven GMC blower, and a Muncie four-speed tranny.

On one of my 1978 trips to Redwood City, I stopped to see Phil Cool and found all these roadsters parked in the driveway. What a sight!

Cool's red '32 had just won the "America's Most Beautiful Roadster" title. The black, flamed roadster in the center was Joe Garcia's beauty. The yellow highboy roadster to the right belonged to Phil Kendrick.

It's funny how spontaneous pictures sometimes turn out well. That's a good enough reason to always keep your camera by your side.

**H**ere's another highly prized, autographed picture from my collection.

Bob Hirohata was the well-known owner of the famous Barris-built chopped-top '51 Mercury. It was uniquely designed with the center posts eliminated between the door and the quarter windows, rendering a hardtop styling.

I believe only two of these autographed pictures exist. Thanks to my good friend Greg Sharp, I have one and he has the other. As you can see, Bob had a sense of humor. He signed it: "Rots of Ruck Andy, Bob Hirohata, 2/22/78 11:15 A.M. PST" (Pacific Standard Time).

Bob Hirohata passed away on May 14, 1981.

**I**n the late 1970s, one of the hottest shows on television was a program called *Charlie's Angels*, starring Kate Jackson, Farrah Fawcett-Majors, and Jaclyn Smith.

Revell, the model car manufacturer, had an idea for a model kit, and wanted someone to build a *Charlie's Angels* van. A Revell public relations company, Promotions Inc., contacted customizer Rod Powell with some design ideas, and soon construction was under way.

Body modifications were done by Henry Hurlhey and Nelson Gong. The front was customized with hefty nerf bars, a custom grille, and Zelmont driving lights from Durimex.

The paint scheme was a Rod Powell original, and he executed it in pink pearl.

The lowering was done by Big Bear Alignment of Salinas, and chrome plating was handled by Salinas Plating. Thrush Performance Products supplied the chrome square tube sidepipes. Goodyear radials were mounted on Cragar mag wheels.

Rocky's Upholstery fashioned the shocking pink upholstery, and a Clarion component stereo system was installed by Salinas Auto Stereo.

The van was displayed throughout the United States for the next three years.

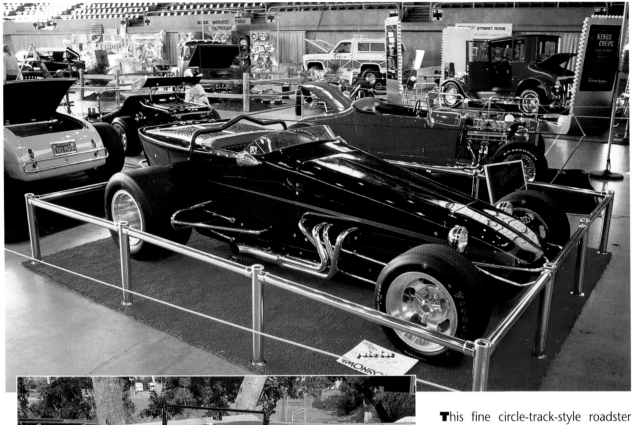

Steve Lawson, of Los Gatos, California, a member of the Bay Area Roadster Club for many years, owned this 1926 T roadster.

This T was originally built by Don Kendall of Costa Mesa, California. The chassis was constructed of 2x3-inch steel tubing. The front suspension had a dropped Super Bell axle, Pete & Jake four-bar wishbones, and '67 Volvo disc brakes.

A 320-ci Ford engine, with Edelbrock Torker intake manifold and a 600-cfm Holley four-barrel carb got things revving. A Ford C-4 automatic transmission was mated to a '73 Ford Maverick rear end with 3.01 gears. The suspension had Jaguar coil-over-shocks and rubber-bushed, four-bar wishbones.

Painted Tru-Spoke wire wheels are fitted with Michelin radial tires.

Greg Morell did the body work and the black acrylic enamel paint. Saddle-tan rolled-and-pleated Naugahyde upholstery was beautifully done by Jim Bailey of Long Beach. Steve Lawson passed away a few years ago.

This fine circle-track-style roadster was owned by Bob Acosta of San Jose, California. When Acosta got the idea for this roadster, he went to Bob Ogden and Mel Wisdom, who built the chassis of 2x3-inch rectangular tubing with four-bar suspension front and rear.

A Speedway Motors 4-inch dropped front axle is tied into VW disc brakes, using a Super Bell kit. The steering unit is Honda Civic rack-and-pinion. The rear end is from a '70 Mustang, with '77 Thunderbird disc brakes adapted for additional stopping power.

A stock 350-ci Chevy engine is linked to a Turbo 350 transmission. The driveshaft is only 8 inches long. Jack Hagemann Jr. fabricated the aluminum body. The black Naugahyde upholstery was the work of Archie Pruitt. Firestone racing tires are mounted on American mag wheels.

Bob Acosta did his own black-lacquer paint with blue scallops. Bob is an Oakland Roadster Show Hall of Fame member.

The *Cool 50* Mercury, originally owned and built by Richard Zocchi of Martinez, California, was owned by Bob Larivee Sr. of Pontiac, Michigan, at the time of this photo in May 1979.

Rod Powell's shop performed some minor body repair, then completely repainted it in this candy-red and silver scheme.

Bill Reasoner of Walnut Creek, California, did the 4 1/2-inch chop top. The front fenders were extended 3 1/2 inches and the headlights were frenched. Those are '53 DeSoto teeth that are fitted into the original Mercury opening. The hood was nosed with the corners rounded, and the peaked scoops were formed in the sides of the hood with three chrome teeth.

A '52 DeSoto bumper is used in front with the bumper bolts cleaned off, and a license plate area cut into center. Side trim is adapted from a '70 Buick Riviera. Ken Foster gets credit for the silver Naugahyde and maroon Mohair interior.

If I told you the nickname of this car is *Deucari,* what would you guess about this custom? How about a deuce roadster with a Ferrari engine? And not just any Ferrari engine, but a V-12!

This car is no Frankenstein, as proved by the "America's Most Beautiful Roadster" award of 1979 from the Oakland Roadster Show.

The 245-ci V-12 is a twin overhead-cam design with three Weber two-barrel carbs. Only a small modification to the deuce Ford was required to accept the engine. The firewall was recessed 3 inches, due to a pair of stock Ferrari distributors.

The transmission is a Muncie four-speed with a modified Hurst shifter. A Halibrand quick-change rear end with 4.30 gears gets the power to the pavement. Other details include '36 Ford axle housings, Koni coil-over-shocks, and disc brakes.

A 4-inch Super Bell dropped front axle, Ford spindles, and VW Type II disc brakes were used up front. And the frame was boxed with a 110-inch wheelbase—4 inches longer than normal, to accommodate the increased length of the Ferrari engine. Jack Hagemann built the three-piece hood and louvered side panels 4 inches longer than stock. The '32 Ford fiberglass body is a product of Westcott's Auto Restyling.

The Indian-red acrylic lacquer paint is arresting, and the V-shaped DuVall windshield is a visual clue that this deuce is something different. The Baroni wire wires have special hubs to accept knock-offs front and rear. A saddle-tan Connolly leather interior with Porsche carpets is conspicuously sumptuous.

This must be one of the most innovative '57 Buick Centurys to ever be customized. The owner, Richard Zocchi of Pittsburg, California, had Rod Powell and Butch Hurlhey chop 3 inches from the top, and french in '76 Cordoba headlights. Custom taillights from a '56 Buick were mounted end to end, and all emblems and door handles were removed.

Other than lowering the Buick, the chassis and engine are stock. Chromed wheels, wide whitewalls, and big Appleton spotlights provide an early-custom styling look. Flawless candy-apple red paint was applied over a silver base by Mike Haas, and silver pinstriping was added by the master, Frank Mills.

Ken Foster did the wide-pleated silver Naugahyde interior, and he dropped the front and rear seats 2 inches for extra headroom.

This photo was taken at the 1979 Oakland Roadster Show.

**H**ere's a rear three-quarter view of the *Jade Idol,* a sectioned '56 Mercury that can be seen from a front view on the title page of this book. It was owned by Jerry Rehn.

The rear quarter panels and a rear grille opening were molded into a single unit with a matching rolled pan. The grille and the bumper were constructed from rectangle tubing to closely resemble the front grille and bumper. Hand-made taillights were installed in the tunneled position.

The trunk remained completely stock. Dual, chromed rectangular exhaust tips protrude on both sides of the nerf-type bumper. Fitted under the fender flares are Buick Skylark wire wheels with Dunlop tires. The engine is a 292-ci Ford Y-block. The interior is upholstered in green velvet and pearl-white Naugahyde.

*Car Craft* magazine named this one of the 10 best customs of 1962. This photo was taken in 1979, as was the one on the title page.

Owner Gary Simon of Montebello, California, called this '29 Ford the *Orange Juice* roadster.

Under the hood is a 302-ci '68 Ford engine backed up by a '68 Ford C4 transmission and a '65 Mustang rear end with 3.08 gears. The upholstery, ginger Naugahyde and nylon, was finished by Modern Auto Upholstery.

The pinstriping of the body moldings, louvers, side panels, splash pans and trunk lid was done by yours truly. I counted 323 louvers. Each was striped twice—once in white and once in black—for a total of 646 brush strokes. It is still a personal record for the most louvers I've ever done on one car.

▮ have discovered that photographing from a few steps higher than eye level gives a more pleasant and a fuller view of the car. This is me photographing Dick Eaton and his '32 Ford roadster on April 7, 1979.

My second camera was mounted on a tripod, and it captured this moment. This picture is a reminder to myself of what I went through to take good pictures.

I laugh about the times I lost my balance and fell off the ladder. It was always embarrassing, but, thankfully, I was never hurt.

**A**nother of my pinstriping subjects was Greg Sharp's '41 Ford pickup. It was painted '75 Corvette bright yellow, and I did the striping in black.

Custom details included a filled cowl vent, de-chroming, and the addition of 72 louvers on the hood and tailgate.

The engine was built by Don Cummins. It's a 327-ci Chevy linked to a 350 Turbo-Hydra-matic transmission and an 8-inch Ford rear end.

"Magoo" did the chassis work, which included the installation of a '65 Chevelle steering unit in conjunction with a '68 Thunderbird tilt-wheel column and shifter. The front axle had a 2 1/2-inch drop.

Currently, Greg's pickup is undergoing another reconstruction by Pete Chapouris and Jim Jacobs at their new So Cal Speed Shop.

This '32 Ford sedan was just a body and frame when George Rasmussen of Palo Alto, California, bought it. The fenders, running boards, and hood were purchased separately.

Gene's Custom Shop of San Jose chopped the top 3 inches, louvered the hood, and painted it in black lacquer. Rod Powell did the yellow-to-orange flames, striping the edges in light blue.

Under the hood is a 327-ci Chevy with a Weiand manifold and Carter AFB carburetor. The transmission is Turbo 350 linked to a '68 Mustang rear end. A '32 front axle is dropped and filled. The front brakes are Volvo discs, and the shocks are '61 Jaguar friction-type units. A '49 Ford donated the steering unit.

Anita Rasmussen is with the sedan in this 1979 photo.

Because we are at the end of the 1970s, and at the end of this book, I want to finish with the 1980 Oakland Roadster Show winner of "America's Most Beautiful Roadster" title.

This 1928 Ford roadster, owned by John Corno, had a 302-ci Ford V-8, with four 48 IDA Weber carbs. The wheels were Center Line Championship rims using Halibrand knock-offs. Porsche-red acrylic lacquer was the paint of choice.

This slick roadster was designed by Harry Bradley and built by John Buttera.

# Index

Acosta, Bob, 115
Adams, Rex, 73
*Aladdin's Dream*, 36
"America's Most Beautiful Roadster" award, 9, 21, 48, 58, 69, 98, 111, 112, 118, 126
Anaheim Show, 64, 65
*Aquarius*, 107
Archer, Arlene, 11
Archer, Steve, 9, 11, 28, 61, 63, 73, 83, 101
Asnicar, Alan, 110
Averill, Neil, 12, 54
Babb, Jim, 28, 63
Bailey, Jim, 115
Bailon, Joe, 14, 32
Banning of Gilroy, 10, 11
Barnes, Bob, 86
Bartnick, Ray, 50
Bay Area/L.A. Roadster Clubs Meet, 63
Bell, Bruce, 41
"Best Appearing Car" award, 20
"Best Closed Car" award, 38
"Best Open" award, 53
"Best Street Rod" trophy, 71
Bethel, Dave, 62
Bethel, Sherrill, 62
*Black Jack*, 59
Boeltl, Lanny, 13
Bonneville National Speed Trials, 19
Boreta, Voss, 24
Bradford, Jack, 89
Bradley, Harry, 70, 89, 126
Brizio, Andy, 9, 10, 14, 28, 36, 74, 83, 107
Brooks, Ron, 79
Broz, Milo, 17
Bryson, Bud, 83
Bryson, Keith, 83
Bucchianeri, Dario, 39
Burgos, Rose, 39
Burgos, Vince, 39
Burnett, Brian, 98
Burnham, Bill, 97
Burton, Bob, 28, 55
Buss, Laura, 100
Buttera, John, 83, 101, 126
Caccia, Howard, 37
*California Lowrider*, 98
*California Touring*, 63
Callejo, Ray, 28, 49
*Candy Man*, 98
Chapouris, Pete, 38, 123
*Charlie's Angels* van, 114
Chrisman, Bob, 63
Clark, Phil, 21
Clausen, Sky, 93
Clenendon, Bill, 39
Colver, Mervin, 64
Conrad, Sam, 19
*Cool 50*, 70, 116
Cool, Phil, 98, 111, 112
Corno, John, 10, 33, 58, 126
Corsello, Chuck, 48
Costa, Harry, 11
Cotta, Tony, 40
Courtney, Ron, 58
Covell, Ron, 44, 61, 93, 101, 104
Cow Palace Car Show, 45
Craig, Dennis, 55, 63
Crisp, Gary, 58
*Crown Coupe*, 64
Cummins, Don, 123
Cunningham, Dave, 55
D'Agostino, John, 21
Daniel, Tom, 61
Davidson, Bob, 69
Davis, Sam, 101, 104
Davis, Steve, 83
DeCruz, Spud, 22
DeMateo, Rocky, 42, 89

DePonzi, Duke, 47
*Deucari*, 118
DeWitt, Bill, 42
Doda, Carol, 24
Dodge, Bob, 67
Dohenick, Dave, 58
Drake, Dennis, 50
Dyar, Bob, 78
Eaton, Dick, 90, 122
Englehart, John, 106
Enslinger, Gary, 45
Epperson, Bob, 11, 49
Erben, Les, 12, 47, 54
Erickson, Eric, 27
Erickson, Mike, 27
Falk, Dick, 55
Farley, Mike, 48, 49, 105
Farrell, Wilson, 12
Fergerson, Pete, 65
Ferreira, Gilbert, 16, 93, 95
Ferreira, Lorraine, 16
Ferreira, Ralph, 15
Fisher, Mel, 12
Foose, Sam, 106
Foster, Ken, 25, 27, 28, 36, 37, 40, 47, 54, 55, 61, 63, 74, 83, 85, 93–95, 107, 111, 116, 120
Foyt, A. J., 98
Fry, Ed, 21, 55
Garcia, Joe, 105, 112
Garcia, Ralph, 57
Gardner, Alice, 37
Gary, Herb, 89
Geyer, Ed, 108
Gilbertson, Gary, 21
Gilbertson, Lonnie, 10, 21, 58, 69
Glaser, Ron, 106
Gong, Nelson, 114
Gorby, Bob, 19
Grabowski, Norm, 32
Guthrie, Janet, 98
Haas, Mike, 21, 27, 40, 55, 120
Haddad, Bob, 79
Hagemann, Jack, 83, 86, 88, 90, 94, 97, 115, 118
Hall, Rhonda, 99
Hawkins, Vic, 26
Henley, Debbrah, 9
Heredia, Rudy, 10
Higgins, Ken, 54
High Performance and Custom Trade Show, 10
Himsl, Art, 9, 21, 28, 37, 55
Himsl, Ellen, 28
Hines, Bill, 62
Hirohata, Bob, 114
Hislop, Lou, 16
Hocker, Tom, 57
Huffman, Bob, 70
Hunter, Jan, 36
Hunter, Vern, 12
Hurlhey, Henry "Butch," 42, 93, 100, 110, 112, 120
*Instant T*, 10, 28
Jacobs, Jim, 38, 123
*Jade Idol*, 121
Jeffords Jr., Bob, 51
Jeffords, JoAnn, 51
*Johnny Lightning 500 Special*, 9
Johnson, Bob, 103
Johnson, Carl, 16
Jones, Bo, 13
Jones, Ron, 78
Jones, Stan, 58
Kane, Dave, 58
Karr, John, 82
Kendall, Don, 115
Kendrick, Phil, 112
Kennedy, Bob, 67
*King's Coupe*, 98
Kraus, Bob, 108
Kugel, Jerry, 84

L.A. Roadster Exhibition, 76, 78
L.A. Roadster Show and Swap Meet, 50
L.A. Roadsters Car Show, 77
*La Jolla*, 89
Laconi, Ron, 22
Lago, Ron, 72
Larivee Sr., Bob, 116
Lawson, Steve, 115
Lee, Ed, 83
Lenz, Ray, 84
Lewis, Paul "Stroker", 100
Lindebaum, Bob, 20
*Little Beaver*, 64
Lodi Mini Nationals, 53–55, 106
Loesch, Wayne, 54
Lohrey, Paul, 41
Los Angeles Winternationals Car Show, 32, 70, 71
Los Angeles/Bay Area Roadster Meet, 20
*Love American Style Machine*, 45
Manger, Bill, 73
Marquez, Wally, 62
Martin, Louie, 72
Martinez, Ed, 19, 62
Martinez, Tony, 84
Mathison, David, 53
McCoy, Bruce, 71
McElley, Paul, 14, 59
McMullen, Tom, 65
Mears, Rick, 98
Megugorac, Dick "Magoo", 18
Mendoza, Bill, 54
Meredith, Mickey, 54
Mierkey, Tom, 38
Miglietto, Dave, 36
Milazzo, Jo, 50
Milazzo, Ray, 50
Mills, Frank, 120
Mitchell, Ted, 30, 43
Moleno, Jim, 98
Monterey Kar Kapades, 73
Morell, Greg, 115
Moses, John, 45
Moyano, Sil, 81
Muller, Lou, 109
Myre, Tom, 64
Nannenhorn, Ken, 98
Nash, Dennis, 72
Navarro, Cathy, 95
Newton, Ed, 32
Nielsen, Jerry, 43, 44
Oakland Roadster Show, 21, 22, 25, 36, 72, 98, 111, 120
*Odyssey*, 40
Ogden, Bob, 115
Ogden, Pete, 25, 40, 55, 61
Ohanesian, Harold "Buddy," 72
*Old Blue*, 97
Old Timer's Rod Run, 53
*Orange Juice* Roadster, 122
Orlando, Pete, 107
Osborn, Guy, 54
Owen, Les, 47
Page, Ivan, 12
Palmer, Joe, 12
"People's Choice," 47
Perez, Joe, 32
Pink Panther promotional car, 32
Pismo Beach Roadster Roundup, 47
*Playbunny Coach*, 27
Powell, Rod, 14, 30, 43, 44, 61, 62, 73, 89, 100, 101, 114, 116, 120, 124
*Praying Mantis*, 50
Prey, Walt, 50
Provost, Albert, 71
Prufer, Tom, 25, 61, 88
Putnam, Dave, 104
Ramos, Nash, 98
Rasmussen, Anita, 67, 124
Rasmussen, George, 66, 67, 124
Reasoner, Bill, 116
Rehn, Jerry, 121

Reid, Don, 67
Reisner, Bob, 32
Rickey, Jack, 52
Rickey, Marilyn, 52
Riggen, Carl, 18
Rio, Lolita, 49
Roach, Bill, 48, 55
Roach, Dale, 55
Roadster Exhibition and Swap Meet, 13
Roadster Roundup, 16, 18
*Roadster, The*, 33
Rock, Tom, 77
Rod & Custom Street Rod Nationals, 10, 28
"Rodder's Choice" award, 41
Rosell, Jerry, 70
Ross, Joe, 73
Rutherford, Johnny, 69
Sacramento Autorama, 26, 98
Salice, Rich, 11
"Sam Barris" award, 26, 48, 70, 98
San Jose Autorama, 59, 85
San Mateo Autorama, 11, 21, 27
Sanchez, Mario, 42
Sanders, Mickey, 56
Santa Barbara Rod Run, 38
Sbarbaro, Bob, 70
Schaffer, Phil, 70
Schoonhover, Bob, 70
Schramek, Ron, 98
Scritchfield, Dick, 19
Seventeen Mile Drive, 84
Sharp, Greg, 33, 76, 114, 123
Siebert, Sonny, 59
Simon, Gary, 122
Smith, Dick, 51, 78
Solimine, George, 15
Southard, Andy, 43, 76
Spangler, Mike, 69
Spence, Christy, 110
Spence, Lee Anna, 110
Spence, Red, 84, 110
Starbird, Darryl, 73
Stich, Jerry, 28, 36, 37, 83, 94, 95
Stryker, Tom, 35
Swanson, Mel, 42
Swenson, Bill, 78
Tabucci, Charlie, 39
Tabucci, Jerry, 39
Thelen, Don, 78
Thelen, Mike, 53
Thompson, Dana, 16
Thompson, Rich, 16
Tremayne, Loren "Curley," 100
Troyer, Jim, 73
Turretto, Greg, 86, 93
Unser, Al, 9, 98
Unser, Bobby, 69
Urbina, Kathleen "Cookie," 49
*Vantasta*, 89
Varner, Don, 85, 86, 101, 104
Varner, Kim, 104
Varni, Dennis, 18
Vasser, Jim, 48, 63
Visalia Roadster Roundup, 19, 20, 40
Vona, Paul, 93
Vrionis, Jerry, 39
Walton, Harold, 58
West Coast Championship Rod Run, 79
Westergard, Harry, 56, 72
White, Connie, 69
White, Vern, 58
Wilde, Willie, 42
Winfield, Gene, 76
Winsett, Butch, 90
Winternationals Car Show, 62
Wisdom, Mel, 115
*Witness, The*, 71
Wright, Debbie, 17
Wussow, Jeff, 20
Wussow, Judy, 20
Zocchi, Richard, 70, 116, 120